The Accompaniment in "Unaccompanied" Bach

Sei Solo.

à Violino senza Basso accompagnato.

Libro Primo.

da

Joh. Seb. Bach.

ao. 1720.

PUBLICATIONS OF THE EARLY MUSIC INSTITUTE

The Accompaniment in "Unaccompanied" Bach

INTERPRETING THE SONATAS AND PARTITAS FOR VIOLIN

Stanley Ritchie

INDIANA UNIVERSITY PRESS
Bloomington & Indianapolis

This book is a publication of

INDIANA UNIVERSITY PRESS
Office of Scholarly Publishing
Herman B Wells Library 350
1320 East 10th Street
Bloomington, Indiana 47405 USA

iupress.indiana.edu

© 2016 by Stanley Ritchie
All rights reserved

frontis:
Autograph page of Bach's "Sei Solo a Violino senza Basso,"
Mus. ms. Bach P 967, fol. 1r. *Courtesy of Staatsbibliothek zu Berlin—
Preußischer Kulturbesitz, Musikabteilung mit Mendelssohn-Archiv.*

No part of this book may be reproduced or utilized in any form or by any means, electronic or mechanical, including photocopying and recording, or by any information storage and retrieval system, without permission in writing from the publisher. The Association of American University Presses' Resolution on Permissions constitutes the only exception to this prohibition.

The paper used in this publication meets the minimum requirements of the American National Standard for Information Sciences—Permanence of Paper for Printed Library Materials, ANSI Z39.48–1992.

Manufactured in the United States of America

Library of Congress Cataloging-in-Publication Data

Names: Ritchie, Stanley, author.
Title: The accompaniment in "unaccompanied" Bach :
interpreting the Sonatas and Partitas for violin / Stanley Ritchie.
Other titles: Publications of the Early Music Institute.
Description: Bloomington ; Indianapolis : Indiana University Press, 2016. | ?2016 |
Series: Publications of the Early Music Institute | Includes bibliographical references.
Identifiers: LCCN 2016010954 (print) | LCCN 2016013161 (ebook) |
ISBN 9780253021984 (print : alkaline paper) | ISBN 9780253022080 (ebook)
Subjects: LCSH: Bach, Johann Sebastian, 1685–1750. Sonaten und Partiten,
BWV 1001–1006. violin, | Violin music—Interpretation (Phrasing, dynamics, etc.)
Classification: LCC MT145.B11 R58 2016 (print) |
LCC MT145.B11 (ebook) | DDC 787.2/183092—dc23
LC record available at http://lccn.loc.gov/2016010954

He played the violin cleanly and penetratingly . . . and understood to perfection the possibilities of all string instruments. This is evidenced by his solos for the violin and for the violoncello without bass. One of the greatest violinists told me once that he had seen nothing more perfect for learning to be a good violinist, and could suggest nothing better to anyone eager to learn, than the said violin solos without bass.

Carl Philipp Emanuel Bach in a letter to
Nicolaus Forkel in December 1774,
trans. Hans T. David and Arthur Mendel.
The New Bach Reader, rev. Christoph Wolff.
New York: Norton, 1998.

Contents

FOREWORD / MAURICIO FUKS   xi
ACKNOWLEDGMENTS   xiii

   Introduction   1

1—**Principles of Interpretation**   5
   Notation   5
   Polyphony   5
   Harmony   6
   Metre   6
   Dynamics   7
   Inequality   7
   Fingering   7
   Note Length   7
   Bow Direction   8
   Articulations   8
   Ornamentation   9

2—**Dance Forms**   10
   Allemanda   10
   Bourée/Borea   11
   Ciaccona   11
   Corrente   11
   Gavotte   12
   Gigue/Giga   12
   Loure   12
   Menuet   13
   Sarabanda/Sarabande   13

Siciliana   14
Double   14
Preludio   14

3 — Analytical Methods and Exercises   16

G-Minor Adagio   17
G-Minor Fuga   20
D-Minor Allemanda   22

4 — The Improvisatory Movements   24

G-Minor Sonata: Adagio   25
A-Minor Sonata: Grave   29

5 — The Fugues   35

G-Minor   35
A-Minor   38
C-Major   42

6 — The Ostinato Movements   46

Partita II: Ciaccona   47
Sonata III: Adagio   53

7 — The Dancelike Movements   57

Bourée and Borea   57
Tempo di Borea   58
B-Minor Corrente   60
D-Minor Corrente   62
Gavotte en Rondeau   64
The Giga   66
The Gigue   68
The Loure   69
The Menuets   71
The Sarabande and Sarabanda   73
The B-Minor Sarabande   73
The D-Minor Sarabanda   74

8—The Virtuoso Movements — 77

G-Minor Sonata: Presto   77
B-Minor Corrente—Double   79
The A-Minor Finale   80
The C-Major *Allegro assai*   82
The E-Major Preludio   84

9—The Philosophical Movements — 87

The Allemanda   87
B-Minor Partita   87
D-Minor Partita   91

10—The Lyrical Movements — 94

The Siciliana   94
A-Minor Sonata: Andante   96
The C-Major Sonata: Largo   97

11—Right-Hand Technique — 100

Polyphony   101
Chordal Technique   101
Martelé and Spiccato   105
Sautillé   106
Bariolage   106
Ondeggiando   108

12—Left-Hand Technique — 109

The Role of Vibrato   110
Half-Position   111
Choice of Fingerings   111
Intonation   113
Tuning   114

Last Words   116

BIBLIOGRAPHY   119

INDEX   121

Foreword

Stanley Ritchie's *Interpreting "Unaccompanied" Bach* is a masterful and comprehensive study of Bach's three Sonatas and three Partitas for solo violin. Professor Ritchie's cultivated and deeply incisive analysis covers all the technical elements and stylistic considerations involved in arriving at a convincing period-style interpretation of these masterpieces—yet, one never feels that his brilliant dissective ability is, as it often can be, a merely challenging intellectual exercise. The ever-present undercurrent of the passion and love Ritchie feels for these works is indeed the dominating and motivating force for this book. I am not a "Baroque" violinist. Nevertheless, I highly recommend this book to *all* violinists—I have no doubt that they will find it, as I have, a source of invaluable information and inspiration.

Mauricio Fuks

Acknowledgments

Writing this book has been a labor of love: studying, performing, and teaching this music have all contributed significantly to my growth as a musician. The decision to write the book was the result, the natural outcome, of my having taught for many years a course in this subject at the Indiana University Jacobs School of Music—the book is a kind of legacy born of a desire to share my conception with a wider audience. It is only fitting, then, that I acknowledge first the help over the years of my students in the course, who have served as guinea pigs—and still do—and provided me with frequent insights and the platform from which to share and test my ideas.

I am most grateful to my editors at Indiana University Press, Raina Polivka and Janice Frisch, who have been so generous with their oversight and their guidance through the postcreative obstacle course. The prompt and courteous assistance of Drs. Martina Rebmann and Roland Schmidt-Hensel of the Berlin Staatsbibliothek, who responded immediately to my request for scanned pages of Bach's autograph, certainly helped to expedite the editing process.

I am indebted to my friends and colleagues, Mauricio Fuks and Joseph Silverstein, who have always been supportive of my work, and to Reinhard Goebel for his perceptive criticism.

Perhaps, though, an expression of posthumous gratitude to Bach himself, the consummate master, is in order: he provided us with an incomparable work of art whose careful study has enriched so many generations of musicians. I do hope he approves of my work.

Introduction

Johann Sebastian Bach's *Sei Solo à Violino senza Basso accompagnato* bears the date 1720. Its uniqueness as an extended example of unaccompanied composition is striking, because there are so few compositions of that genre that have come down to us from that period and none of such scope. Heinrich von Biber's *Passacaglia* from the *Rosenkrantz Sonaten* of 1675, which bears great similarity to Bach's *Ciaccona*, and Johann Paul von Westhoff's unaccompanied *Suite* (1683) and *Partitas* (1696) each predate Bach's pieces by decades. Johann Georg Pisendel's *Sonata à Violino Solo senza Basso*, itself a substantial example of early eighteenth-century virtuosity, is thought to have been composed a few years earlier. Each of these demonstrates the advanced state of polyphonic composition in the German school of violin playing in the time of Bach. Whereas the Italians had previously shown the way, even with the introduction of polyphony by composers such as Biagio Marini in his *Sonate, Symphoniae . . . Op. 8* (1626), and Carlo Farina—*Il quarto Libro delle Pavane, Gagliarde . . . Sonate, Canzon à 2, 4* (1628)—it was the Germans who explored and exploited the polyphonic possibilities of the instrument. The final, ingenious work in Biber's 1681 set at first glance appears to be a trio sonata with two individual parts on separate staffs: these are, however, to be played by one violinist. There is ongoing speculation as to the influence the music of all these composers may have had on Bach, even as to the possibility that he was familiar with Pisendel's sonata, which certainly cannot be ruled out, but if one examines Johann Jakob Walther's monumental *Hortulus Chelicus* (1688/1694), even though the pieces in this particular collection have figured bass accompaniment, one cannot help but be struck by the similarity of the chordal writing.

Apart from the polyphonic influence of the German school, though, one may detect other similarities, such as the arpeggiated episodic passages in the fugues that recall variations in the sonatas of Schmelzer and Biber, and the climactic thirty-second-note passage in the first part of the *Ciaccona*, which has its counterpart in the music of Biber and Walther. The E-major Partita is an interesting combination of national tastes: the Preludio has a distinctly Vivaldian flavor, and the subsequent dance-like movements are clearly inspired, as with the work of other contemporary German composers, by the *ordres* of the French school. Describing Bach's compositional style as eclectic, the product of the compilation of various national influences—German, French, and Italian—has long since become a cliché. However, this does not prevent us from marveling at his ability to synthesize them and to produce something so unique, an individual compositional language that was the last word in the evolution of unaccompanied violin writing for the next two centuries.

For whom, then, did Bach write these pieces? It seems unreasonable to assume that they were merely an exercise in composition. This is a question for which, in the absence of a dedicatory preface, we shall probably never have a definite answer. However, it is possible that they were for Pisendel, who, as concertmaster in the court of Dresden, was the reigning virtuoso in the region. Whatever the truth is, that he himself was an excellent violinist is indisputable: in a letter to Johann Nicolaus Forkel, his father's biographer, Carl Philipp Emanuel stated that "he played the violin cleanly and penetratingly" and that he "understood to perfection the possibilities of all stringed instruments."[1] Whereas the Sonatas and Partitas were not published in his lifetime, though, and were comparatively unknown until the nineteenth century, they were already mentioned in correspondence and writing of the period as being valuable pedagogical material. Forkel, writing in 1802, reported that "for a long series of years, the violin solos were universally regarded by the greatest performers on the violin as the best means to make an ambitious student a perfect master of his instrument."[2]

Three centuries later, these works are still used as vehicles for the development of technique and, as such, are standard curricular requirements in most music schools. They nevertheless comprise some of the most controversial of repertoire, and in my experience, discussions of their interpretation are generally avoided by violinists who have not immersed themselves in the music of composers preceding and contemporary with Bach. In the past half century, however, a remarkable development, the intensive archaeological research into performance practices of all music, has enabled us to reexamine concepts of execution and to reconstruct in detail the stylistic norms of the various periods and nationalities.

What I intend to set down in these pages is a rational approach to the interpretation of this unique musical genre. The language of Johann Sebastian Bach is supremely logical, and in that logic reside clues to tempi, dynamics, and expression—in short, all of the information necessary to enable the performer to arrive at an interpretation that accords with concepts of good taste and style as understood at the time the music was composed. But how are we to define these? It's obvious that even though we do our homework, studying all of the relevant performance practice literature, primary and secondary, the conclusions we reach can only be subjective, which is as true now as it has always been, for even in Bach's time, differing interpretations

---

1. From a letter from Carl Phillip Emanuel Bach to Forkel quoted on p. 397 of *The New Bach Reader* (New York: Norton, 1998).
2. Johann Nicolaus Forkel, *Über Johann Sebastian Bachs Leben, Kunst und Kunstwerke* (Leipzig: 1802).

were surely the norm. It is impossible, therefore, to postulate any interpretation as the only "correct" one.

On the other hand, there are ways to approach Baroque music that are distinctly different from the traditional "Romantic" style. If we wish to try to experience as closely as possible the day-to-day life of the eighteenth-century musician, we may start by eliminating certain characteristic elements of modern playing: the Tourte bow, the chin rest, constant vibrato, and *martelé* and *spiccato* bow strokes; then we can take advantage of wide-ranging research by specialists in the many aspects of performance practice and apply various ornamental devices, choose appropriate tempi, capture the characteristic lilt of Baroque dances, understand rhetorical principles, and so on, thereby moving, albeit artificially, in the direction of a seventeenth- or eighteenth-century aesthetic. For those who are curious about Baroque style but find this approach too extreme and are unwilling to forgo the familiarity of the modern instrument, it is still possible, in consultation with source materials, to approximate the experience of the "authenticists." By these means, we may move away from the traditional, but what lies beyond is largely guesswork.

But is this not true of all music? Do we really know how nineteenth-century performers played? To be sure, there are many descriptions—eyewitness accounts—of various Romantic virtuosi performing, and some recordings exist, but the style of playing varied considerably: if we seek to postulate a "correct" Romantic style, we're doomed to disappointment. The various schools of violin playing in the nineteenth and twentieth centuries have their well-documented parallel in the seventeenth and eighteenth centuries, though, and the information in contemporary source material can help us greatly in our quest to understand how musicians then may have played, according to where and when they lived.

Conservatory-style musical training tends to rely upon tradition, whereby the student is provided with ready-made interpretations, music completely fingered and bowed, and perhaps with one's teacher's instructions to listen to a particular recording in order to determine the accepted tempi, dynamics, and nuances. Have we not all been there? Of course, prior to the end of the eighteenth century, composers provided very few written or symbolic indications of expression, so that musicians of our time have become dependent on heavily edited versions of the standard Baroque and Classical repertoire, more often than not the work of soloists, that pass down interpretative ideas that may have little to do with the style and spirit of the music as understood by the composer. This is the "traditional" approach—institutionalized pedagogical laziness—and, as a result, we, as students, are taught interpretations but not *the art of interpreting*.

Until the end of the eighteenth century, musicians were trained to read expression in the notes themselves: oral traditions passed down from master to pupil were periodically codified in treatises and method books, which now stand as milestones in the evolutionary process. What led to the practice of the systematic annotation of expression, though, had to do with the breaking, by composers such as Carl Philipp Emanuel Bach, of established rules—the insertion of unusual dynamics and nuances—that eventually resulted in the necessity to provide *all* expression marks, the normal and the hitherto extraordinary. Unfortunately, to a considerable degree, the creative interpretative rights of the performer were thereby abrogated.

There are excellent books by eminent scholars that treat this subject in great detail. I am, however, a violinist, not a musicologist; a teacher, not a researcher; I am a performer who has spent some forty-five years playing Baroque and Classical music on period instruments, and more than thirty of them on the faculty of the Indiana University Jacobs School of Music, sharing my experience with young people similarly drawn by curiosity into the field of historically informed performance. This book, then, is an expression of what I believe to be a reasonable, practical approach to a style of music making with which Bach's contemporaries would have been familiar.

In my organization of the book, I have chosen to categorize similar movements, grouping them together rather than treating each complete work in its own separate chapter, as is the more customary way. It is my belief that comparing similar movements, which this facilitates, draws attention to their individual characteristics and to how one varies from another.

This book is not aimed exclusively at "historical" students and performers: it is my hope that all players may find in these pages information that helps them to become fluent in the language of music composed before the advent of prescribed expression, thus opening the way to interpretations that reflect and are in accordance with principles understood by our colleagues in Bach's time. I encourage you, in particular, to experiment with the analytical exercises prescribed in chapter 2, even if only mentally, and if you're curious about how I myself apply the ideas that I share with you, you may want to listen to my own CD of these pieces: *Sei Solo à Violino senza Basso accompagnato*: Musica Omnia—MO0503.

CHAPTER ONE

Principles of Interpretation

My purpose in this opening chapter is to summarize information about various aspects of the topic, which will be alluded to throughout the book and provide the basis for clearer understanding of ideas that may frequently be novel or at odds with contemporary concepts of interpretation.

Notation

My suggestions for interpretation are based on the use of the facsimile of Bach's autograph, with occasional reference to the copy by Anna Magdalena. Once one becomes used to reading it, the notation in both manuscripts is fairly clear, and if one is to arrive at an independent interpretation, their use is essential. Bear in mind that any "Urtext" edition has involved decision making on the part of the editor, whose task it is to decipher the numerous ambiguities. One of my goals in writing this book is to help readers in this process in the hope of liberating them from reliance on editions of any kind.

We should also be aware that any system of notation represents the closest possible approximation to the composer's intention, and that it was only in the twentieth century that composers began to micromanage, even to the extent of dictating the duration of notes. It is important, therefore, to familiarize oneself with certain conventions spelled out in treatises of the period that have to do with rhythmic alteration and rubato. Since the only information we're given is the notes themselves, we must learn to read between the lines.

Polyphony

Examination of the facsimile will reveal an important feature:

Bach never wrote two notes on one stem.

This notational convention clearly shows that Bach was always thinking polyphonically. Hence, a double-stop, or a three- or four-voice chord should never be perceived as a vertical entity except for the purpose of harmonic identification: it is a point at which the separate voices coincide. The concept of vocal coincidence helps us to give each line its appropriate weight, according to whether its function is primary or accompanying.

Harmony

Awareness of the function of each chord—whether consonant or dissonant—and the nature of the harmonic progressions is essential to determining the dynamic shape of gestures and phrases, and consequently the organization of the music. Generally speaking, a dissonance will resolve on a consonance and be dynamically stronger, but as with most generalizations, you will encounter occasional exceptions according to context. I point out to my students that we, in the twenty-first century, have heard everything—or think we have—but if we are to react to music as eighteenth-century musicians did, we need to be surprised by and respond to harmonies such as the diminished-seventh chord that are familiar to us but novel or even shocking to them.

Metre

The metre of a movement is an essential factor in the determination of its tempo. One of my cardinal rules of interpretation is that *all music is in one*, by which I mean that there is one strong beat per measure and one weak, an ancient practice referred to as *tactus*. This concept enables us to differentiate between similar metres—$\frac{2}{4}$ and $\frac{4}{4}$, $\frac{6}{8}$ and $\frac{12}{8}$—and to understand why a composer chose one rather than the other. In the case of triple metres, in which the "tactus" will be irregular, the irregularity will be dictated by the sequence of harmonies, sometimes *one-two*, sometimes *one-three*, but only rarely *one-two-three* even when there are three different chords.

In principle, then, when a composer has chosen $\frac{2}{4}$ over $\frac{4}{4}$, the eighth-note, which is a subdivision in $\frac{4}{4}$, is the basic unit in $\frac{2}{4}$. The affect will usually be more energetic, and the tempo at times relatively slower, due to the frequency of strong beats. Indeed, Bach's puzzling use of $\frac{2}{4}$ as the metre of the B-minor Tempo di Borea, notated as four quarter-notes per measure, might be interpreted as his way of indicating a moderate tempo, for there are certainly two strong beats in many bars.

Alla breve, or "cut time," a term that refers to there being one strong beat per two measures, is usually indicated symbolically. However, it is important to recognize that more often than not, throughout the Sonatas and Partitas, the second bar of a pair is weaker harmonically, thereby creating what is essentially *alla breve*. Note also how Bach chose $\frac{3}{4}$ with half bar-lines as the metre in the G-minor Presto and for the B-minor Corrente—a type of *alla breve*—but with normal, full bar-lines for the Double of the latter, which has the effect of holding that section in check despite the tempo mark of *presto*.

Dynamics

The dynamic structure of the music is governed by several factors:

> the overall architecture of the movement
> the prevailing affect
> the alternation of consonance and dissonance
> *tessitura* (the vertical range of pitches)
> linear direction
> the use of rhetorical devices

Although symbolic dynamic indications are rare in Baroque music, becoming familiar with composers' use of the features I have listed will lead to a better understanding of appropriate concepts of expression. Each of these topics will be referred to at times in the course of the book.

Inequality

The Baroque concept of inequality—"good" and "bad" notes, strong and weak syllables, dissonance and resolution, the subdivision of beats and measures into stressed and unstressed elements—applies throughout and is an essential aspect of effective interpretation. In certain contexts, the concept also applies to rhythm, especially in French music, where a series of eighth-notes may be played with long-short inequality, not unlike the jazz tradition of "swinging," to enhance the flow. So-called *Lombardic* (short-long) rhythm will occasionally be applied as an ornamental variation of "straight" notes. The practice is discussed at length in chapter 7 in the section on the Minuet.

Fingering

The polyphonic nature of the music demands great clarity, and for this reason it's best to favor fingerings in low positions unless higher ones are specifically implied or unavoidable. It is best, also, not to run up to third and fourth position in order to avoid string crossings, which are often much more desirable musically, and technically quite practicable, especially when using a period bow. This topic is treated in detail in chapter 12.

Note Length

Clarity of voice-leading requires careful control of note length so as to avoid confusion. For instance, there will usually be one accompanying note in a double-stop and one melodic, and even though they may be identically notated, the melodic note should generally be held longer than the accompanying one. (An exception is to be found in a passage such as mm. 156–160 of the A-minor Fuga, where two voices move in parallel sixths.)

Bow Direction

Many passages are most effective when bowed "as it comes," because the use of repeated up-bows often draws attention to notes that are relatively unimportant. Neither is it essential to play a strong beat with a down-bow, even when it occurs on a three- or four-note chord. In principle, of course, it is better to use bow direction in accordance with the harmonic context (i.e., with a down-bow on a strong harmony resolving to an up-bow), but this will not always be possible. One frequently encounters passages in which the best effect is to be found in the use of bow direction that may seem counterintuitive: Bach does indeed expect one to bow in reverse at times, and bowing "as it comes" often produces a much more satisfactory reading. In "three-and-one" passages, one should avoid the use of the "hook-stroke," which has the simultaneous undesirable effects of flattening texture and reducing resonance. It is, of course, a variety of *martelé*—short, stopped strokes—which did not become a part of normal right-arm technique until the nineteenth century.

Articulations

Articulation in speech or music may be defined as the separation of one sound from another: in musical terms *an articulation*, or "sound," can refer to a single note or else two or more notes under a slur. In eighteenth-century music, a slur should be treated as a type of ornament—not a technical suggestion that may be altered at the whim or for the convenience of the performer. Because of our training, it is normal to perceive slurs as "bowings," and therefore changeable when inconvenient or awkward; in eighteenth-century music, nothing could be further from the truth. In Bach's music, slurs create variety of texture and are an important part of the language and reflect the aesthetic ideals of his time. In attempting to arrive at an interpretation that does justice to his intentions, one should remember that by all accounts Bach was a fine violinist, and start by following the markings he provided.

At times, the precise length of a slur is difficult to determine, and one must make an artistic decision about the number of notes it encompasses. In Bach's manuscript, many slurs are quickly and imprecisely drawn, as if to say, "It's obvious what I mean—I don't need to waste time being careful." On the other hand, there are instances where he goes to great pains to ensure that his intention is unmistakable. When encountering a slur that could be read in various ways, weigh the choices both musically and technically: more often than not, the musically desirable solution will also turn out to be violinistically logical.

Finally, one difference between modern notation and that of Bach's time is that then a slur from a pair of tied notes would always start from the second note of the tie. Because of this, if there is ambiguity, always consider the possibility that subsequent notes should be taken in the same direction as the tie.

Ornamentation

Well into the nineteenth century, performers were expected to be able to add improvised ornaments to the basic musical text, even to the extent of providing concerto cadenzas *ex tempore*. In some repertoire, notably French Baroque, all the ornaments were prescribed by the composer, leaving no room for spontaneous improvisation. At the other end of the spectrum, the slow movements of the Sonatas for Violin and Continuo, op. 5, of Corelli provided simple melodic lines on which a performer was expected to improvise spontaneously. When Bach's slow movements—which are essentially written-out examples of the combination of French and Italian ornamentation referred to as *les goûts réunis*—became known, a controversy erupted. Johann Adolph Scheibe, a composer and theorist, criticized its use as excessive and was immediately attacked for his views by contemporary composers and aestheticians.[1] Chief among Scheibe's complaints were that in composing a completely ornamented work, Bach had obscured the simple melodic lines, and that the work of improvisation was that of the performer, not the composer. Be that as it may, what we have as a result is a unique historical document: a brilliant example of Bach's own improvisatory style. In my opinion, then, the two movements that I classify as improvisatory should subtly reflect the tradition on which they were based, with the notation understood as descriptive, not prescriptive.

What Bach did so exquisitely was take two dissimilar ornamental styles—the Italian: florid gestures that connect basic melodic notes; and the French: symbolically notated embellishments of individual notes—and meld them into a style uniquely his own. I discuss in detail his use of ornaments and suggest ways of reading them at various times throughout the volume.

---

1. For a detailed account, see George Buelow's biographical article on Scheibe in *Grove Music Online*.

CHAPTER TWO

Dance Forms[1]

Dance was an essential element of court life in eighteenth-century Europe, and whereas none of Bach's Partita movements was intended for use as ballroom accompaniment, we should bear in mind that knowledge of the characteristics and appropriate tempi of the various dances is essential if we seek to approximate their style. As esoteric as this may sound, three centuries later, we now have access to and may profit from the fruits of considerable research by experts in this field in order to have a glimpse of that fascinating social ritual. I recommend to my students that they at least watch videos, if not live performances, of Baroque dances reconstructed by soloists and troupes that specialize in this art, and, better still, that they avail themselves of any opportunity to experience Baroque dance personally in a workshop setting. The physical sensation of Baroque dance can have a remarkable and lasting effect on the way one uses the bow when playing these movements.

Allemanda

This was one of the most popular of Baroque instrumental dances and a standard movement, along with the *Courante, Sarabande,* and *Gigue,* of the suite. The *Allemande* originated some time in the early or mid-sixteenth century, appearing under such titles as "Teutschertanz" or "Dantz" in Germany and "bal todescho," "bal francese," and "Tedesco" in Italy. Originally a moderate duple-metre dance in two or three strains, the Allemande came to be one of the most highly stylized of all Baroque dances. However, because it is more in the nature of an *Entrée*, an introductory processional piece, and lacks the rhythmic energy and regularity of other dances, I have chosen to categorize it instead as a philosophical movement and discuss it in chapter 9. This is in accord with the opinion of influential eighteenth-century commentators.

---

1. Much of the description and historical information in this chapter is adapted from Meredith Little and Natalie Jenne's *Dance and the Music of J. S. Bach* (Bloomington: Indiana University Press, 1991), 35–46, and from various articles in *Grove Music Online*.

Bourée/Borea

During the reign of Louis XIV, the *Bourée* came into fashion both as a social dance at balls and as a theatrical dance. Lully included Bourées in many of his ballets and operas, and composed one for the dancing-lesson scene in Act 1 of Molière's *Le bourgeois gentilhomme* (1670). Later French composers for the stage, including Charpentier, Destouches, Campra, and Rameau, continued to use Bourées in dancing scenes and occasionally in overtures.

As stylized dance music, the Bourée was characterized by duple metre with an upbeat of a quarter-note, a moderate to fast tempo (half-note = *c*80–92) and phrases built out of four-bar units. Bourée choreographies are fairly simple in comparison to other dances like the Sarabande, Gigue, and Loure: they are light, carefree, energetic, and fleet.

Ciaccona

A form of continuous variation similar to the *Passacaglia*, which became popular during the Baroque era, the Chaconne originated in Latin America in the late sixteenth century as a lively dance which had both instrumental and vocal accompaniment. Although no music for the Latin American type survives, it is most likely that the refrain was constructed on one of a number of typical harmonic patterns. During the early seventeenth century, the Chaconne appeared in Spain and Italy, where it became popular as both a dance and an instrumental form. The Chaconne also became popular in France and, toward the middle of the seventeenth century, in Germany and England. In France, the dance became slower and statelier, as did the *Sarabande* on its removal to France from Spain.

It is interesting to note that Bach subtly transforms his *Ciaccona* into a *Passacaglia* at the twenty-fourth measure and proceeds thereafter to go back and forth between the two forms throughout the movement. I shall deal with that feature at length in chapter 6.

Corrente

A fast triple-metre dance and instrumental form popular from the late sixteenth century until the mid-eighteenth century, it is usually considered by some to be an Italian version of the *Courante*. However, whereas the normal metre of the elegant Courante is $\frac{3}{2}$, Bach's *Corrente* is in $\frac{3}{4}$, and, as one of the standard dances in a partita, a vehicle for idiomatic display.

Gavotte

Like most Baroque dances, the *Gavotte* was used as both an instrumental and a vocal air as well as for dancing. Johann Mattheson claimed that it expressed "triumphant joy," an affect that certainly fits the character of Bach's E-major Gavotte.[2] In the first half of the eighteenth century, it was one of the most popular instrumental forms derived from a dance, frequently forming part of keyboard and instrumental suites, where it usually appeared after the more serious movements (*Allemande, Courante, Sarabande*, but in this case, the *Loure*), along with other popular dances like the Minuet and the Bourée.

Gigue/Giga

This is one of the most popular of Baroque instrumental dances and a standard movement, along with the Allemande, Courante, and Sarabande, of the suite. It apparently originated in the British Isles, where popular dances and tunes called "jig" have been known since the fifteenth century. During the seventeenth century, distinct French and Italian styles emerged. The French Gigue was written in a moderate or fast tempo ($^6_4$, $^3_8$, or $^6_8$) with irregular phrases. The Italian *Giga* sounded much faster than the French Gigue but had a slower harmonic rhythm; it was usually in $^{12}_8$ time and marked "presto," with balanced four-bar phrases and a homophonic texture. From about 1690, Gigues and Gigas appeared that were highly complex virtuoso solo pieces which used a wide variety of compositional techniques, usually with joyful affect.

The Italian Giga is particularly associated with violin music, with its characteristic chordal figurations and large melodic leaps, and many *Gighe* occur as last movements in Italian solo and trio sonatas by composers such as Corelli, Veracini, Geminiani, and Tartini. The Giga was adopted by some French composers—notably J. M. Leclair and Mondonville—and by such Germans as Reincken, Telemann, Handel, and J. S. Bach.

The two movements of this type in Bach's solo Partitas bear a striking resemblance to each other, the main difference being the choice of metre—$^{12}_8$ in the D-minor Giga versus $^6_8$ in the E-major—which is most probably an indication of tempo, whereby the Giga might be played faster than the Gigue.

Loure

The eighteenth-century *Loure* was usually a slow, virtuoso French theater dance of a noble, majestic, but languid character, often associated with the pastoral tradition. The Loure was often described as a slow Gigue or "Spanish Gigue," but it was also associated with the *Entrée* in its complex solo choreography and majestic affect. The music of Bach's E-major Loure is indeed similar to that of a slow Gigue, set in $^6_4$ time,

---

2. Johann Mattheson, *Der vollkommene Kappelmeister* (Hamburg, 1739).

using phrases of irregular length, and characteristic motifs such as the dotted figure typical of the Gigue and the eighth-note-quarter-note upbeat. Bach also arranged the piece for lute with different ornamentation.

Menuet

One of the most popular social dances in aristocratic society from the mid-seventeenth century to the late-eighteenth century, the Minuet was dignified, graceful, relaxed, and unaffected. The attention of both dancers and spectators was directed to the elegant and seemingly effortless performance of Minuet step-units, each consisting of four tiny steps in $\frac{6}{4}$ time set in counter-rhythm to two bars of music in $\frac{3}{4}$. The basic unit of the dance is two bars long (not one or four), and while dancers' movements always imply an accent on the first beat of a unit, the downbeat of the second is usually weak. The essential Minuet characteristics are a moderate tempo, and an intimate and nonchalant affect, such as simple joy or peace. Indeed, much has been written about the tempo of the Minuet, both in the eighteenth century and in modern times: the large number of conflicting treatises and studies suggests that there was no fixed tempo for this dance over the centuries, but considerable variety in the different courts and cities in which the Minuet was performed.

Sarabanda/Sarabande

A dance popular from the late sixteenth century to the eighteenth century—as an instrumental form, it was one of the principal movements of the Baroque suite, in which it usually followed the *Courante*. Like the *Chaconne*, it originated in Latin America (where it was accompanied by song, castanets, and guitars) and appeared in Spain during the sixteenth century. During this period, it was a fast, lively dance alternating between $\frac{3}{4}$ and $\frac{6}{8}$ metre and with a reputation for lasciviousness: Father Mariana (1536–1624) in his *Treatise against Public Amusements* speaks of it as "a dance and song so loose in its words and so ugly in its motions that it is enough to excite bad emotions in even very decent people." In 1583, Philip II suppressed the dance in Spain, but still it managed to flourish.

In the early seventeenth century the *Sarabande* was introduced to Italy, whence the first notated examples survive as tablatures for the Spanish guitar. It soon spread to France, where it appeared in the *Ballet de cour* and other theatrical entertainments, as well as in the ballroom, and it was here that the much slower and statelier version of the dance evolved. This was in triple time with a clear emphasis on the second beat, which was often dotted.[3] This form of Sarabande appears in the works of many French composers, including Chambonnières, the Couperins, D'Anglebert, and Rameau, and was also the preferred style among such German composers as Bach, in whose B-minor Partita it is provided with a *Double*.

---

3. Note that this feature is more evident in choreography than in Bach's two movements of this type. See the discussion in chapter 7.

Siciliana

This is a term commonly used to refer to an aria type and instrumental movement popular in the late seventeenth and eighteenth centuries, when it often referred to a dance commonly considered a form of slow Gigue. It rapidly gained popularity in the late seventeenth century and was much used as an aria type in the operas of Alessandro Scarlatti and his contemporaries. In the eighteenth century, the *Siciliana* was associated with pastoral scenes and melancholy emotions, and it is thought to be the basis for the Christmas carol, *Stille Nacht*. It was as a dance, however, that the Siciliana was known to eighteenth-century theorists. Brossard (*Dictionaire de musique*, 1703) described the "canzonette siciliane" as a kind of Gigue, with its $\frac{6}{8}$ or $\frac{12}{8}$ metre and the characteristic dotted eighth-note-sixteenth-note-eighth-note figure on downbeats (he elsewhere described the figure as "*in saltarello*"). Mattheson (*Das neu-eröffnete Orchestre*, 1713) linked it with the *Napolitana* and the *Barcarolle*, suggesting that it was to be performed slowly and was best used to evoke melancholy passions. Since the metre of the one in Bach's G-minor Sonata is $\frac{12}{8}$, though, it ought not to be played too slowly but in an easily flowing tempo. Because of its aria-like character, I have chosen to discuss it in chapter 10, "The Lyrical Movements."

Double[4]

This is a French term used during the seventeenth and early eighteenth centuries for a technique of variation in which more or less elaborate ornamentation is added to the original melody, while the supporting harmonies remain the same. In his first Partita, Bach used the device to add an element of virtuosity, thereby amplifying the affect of each movement.

Preludio[5]

This is a term of varied application that, in its original usage, indicated a piece that preceded other music whose tonic, mode, or key it was designed to introduce; was instrumental (the root *ludus* means "played" as opposed to "sung"); and was improvised (hence the French *préluder* and the German *präludieren*, meaning "to improvise"). The term *"praeambulum"* (preamble) adds the rhetorical function of attracting the attention of an audience and introducing a topic. The earliest notated preludes are for organ and were used to introduce vocal music in church. Slightly later ones, for other chordal instruments such as the lute, grew out of improvisation and were a means of checking the tuning of the instrument and the quality of its tone, and of loosening the player's fingers.

---

4. Greer Garden, "Double," *Grove Music Online. Oxford Music Online* (Oxford: Oxford University Press), accessed January 11, 2015.
5. David Ledbetter, "Prelude," *The New Grove Dictionary of Opera* (2001).

In violin literature, a tradition of "preluding" emerged in seventeenth-century England, with composers such as Matteis preceding suites with an unaccompanied movement of this genre.[6] With Bach, in the suites for violin and cello, and in his keyboard works, the prelude reached the pinnacle of its development, both in its compositional quality and in its range of styles, manners, and formal prototypes. One might also consider the first movement of each violin sonata as a prelude to the Fuga, even though none is so labeled. Interestingly, Bach also used the E-major Prelude as the introductory organ Sinfonia, with orchestral accompaniment, to his Cantata *Wir danken dir, Gott, wir danken dir*, BWV 29.

---

6. Nicola Matteis, "Ayres for the Violin" (London: 1676, 1685).

CHAPTER THREE

Analytical Methods and Exercises

A trap into which one can fall all too easily when studying one of the Sonatas or Partitas for the first time, or when returning to it, is imitating a favorite recorded performance. This is a shame, because there is so much that one can glean from the music itself, especially from the facsimile, in the creation of one's own personal interpretation. Ideally, the first step is to sit down without the instrument and read through the particular movement, hearing its harmonic structure and discerning its architecture. This is where a fairly simple analytical process helps.

The literal meaning of the word *analysis*—"a breaking up"—aptly describes the process by which we may gain insight into the complex yet logical structure of Bach's solo violin compositions. In this chapter, I shall provide a set of analytical exercises designed to separate the music into component parts, the better to understand its harmonic and melodic structure.

First, though, let us consider an important fact. The title of these works, *Sei Solo a Violino senza Basso accompagnato*, is somewhat misleading, for "Basso Accompagnato" merely refers to the customary support of the solo voice by continuo accompaniment on a keyboard, stringed, or plucked instrument. However, because there is no continuo part, the accompaniment is skillfully woven into the solo texture. In the preamble to my course entitled "The Interpretation of Unaccompanied Bach," therefore, I announce to the class that this is a course about something that does not exist:

There is no such thing as "unaccompanied" Bach.

Players of treble instruments tend to focus their attention on the upper line to the neglect of the bass, and consequently to overlook its significance in supporting harmonic progressions, which shape the music dynamically and control the expression. The bass line is therefore the most important element in any Baroque composition, and the performer must be aware of it at all times, for it is the foundation of the music's harmonic structure. It is also essential to be able to identify the simple melodic lines embedded in Bach's often-florid text. In this chapter I use excerpts from various movements to demonstrate analytical methods that help us understand his logic.

G-Minor Adagio

Using as an example the opening measures of the G-minor Sonata, the first exercise I give my class is the identification and extraction of the bass line. The parentheses in m. 3 show that the E-flat is to be heard as the bass note even though it is only touched on briefly in mid-melisma.[1]

Note that, for analytical purposes, the length of the bass notes indicates the duration of the particular harmony: Bach's are shorter mainly for compositional reasons: the bass notes are frequently unplayable as written, but to me they indicate the degree of energy at the moment—the shorter, the more energetic.

The next analytical step is the addition of figures to identify the harmonies:

---

1. I discuss the controversial E-natural on beat three of m. 3 in chapter 4, "The Improvisatory Movements."

And next, the reduction of the melodic line, by removal of ornamental notes, to a simple version such as one finds, for instance, in Corelli's op. 5 sonatas:

Due to a common misperception among violinists that the highest voice is always the most important, when it is frequently only a descant line, one often hears this bizarre rendition of m. 2:

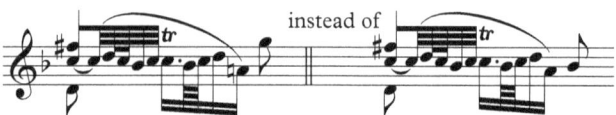

This is quite incorrect, for the F-sharp in the soprano leads to the G, a descant voice, while the alto—the principal voice—moves from the C, through the cadential ornament, to resolve on the melodic B-flat. Written note lengths should never be read as absolute: just as it is impossible to play the first chord of the Adagio as it appears—sustaining all four quarter-notes for their full value—neither is it necessary to sustain notes for their written value simply because it's possible, which can result in ambiguity and confusion. Hence, the correct way to render the chord on the third quarter of m. 2 is to roll quickly up to the sixth (G/B-flat), not leaving the A-string, and then release the G so that the B-flat continues alone.

A simple general rule is that in any vocal coincidence the primary melodic voice should be sustained longer than its accompanying neighbor. Here are two of the many instances in which ignoring this rule can cause confusion:

Whereas this is an analytical exercise, for practical purposes it is essential that the performer be constantly aware of the bass line, for the prevailing bass note will often suggest a nuance that might otherwise be overlooked. One excellent example of the importance of this awareness occurs in m. 19:

Excerpt from the Adagio of the Sonata in G-moll of Bach's "Sei Solo a Violino senza Basso," Mus. ms. Bach P 967, fol. 2r. *Courtesy of Staatsbibliothek zu Berlin—Preußischer Kulturbesitz, Musikabteilung mit Mendelssohn-Archiv.*

The downbeat of the second bar is frequently played as a triad with an open D, but what resembles D is actually the flag of the sixteenth-note A. Whoever was originally responsible for this error evidently failed to understand that Bach never wrote two notes on the same stem, as his music is polyphonic and each note in a chord is part of a separate vocal line.

In this instance, when one is aware of the C on the third beat being the start of a continuous (though inaudible) pedal tone for three quarter-notes, the gesture on the second downbeat has a much stronger flavor: it has the nature of a rhetorical question, and because of the ninth between the imaginary bass note C and the soprano D, a very real tension exists at this moment. The subsequent phrase may then be subtly delayed and played in a more subdued way, falling away to the cadence:

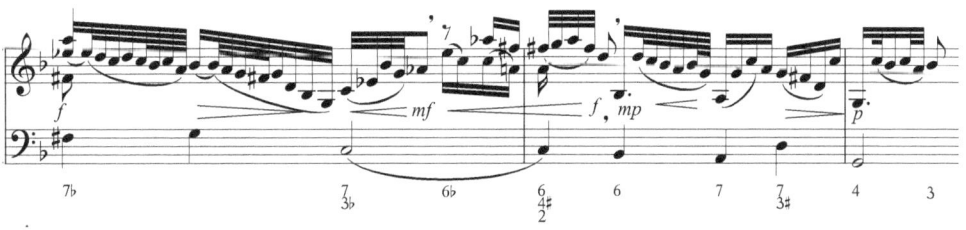

G-Minor Fuga

In the following analysis of the first episode, I have indicated the duration of harmonic units with commas and beam breaks. It is also important to shape the individual elements dynamically, as demonstrated, but to treat the division into phrasing units with subtlety so as to be virtually imperceptible.

Hearing such passages chordally is essential to understanding the voice leading:

A further benefit, though, is that focusing primarily on the relatively slow-moving harmonic and melodic motion encourages a more spacious rendition with due attention to detail.

The following analysis of the last half bar of sixteenth-notes, when the three voices are extracted, reveals a Baroque cliché, a 7–6 progression leading to a half cadence that paves the way to a triumphal statement of the subject. 7–6 and 4–3 progressions, ubiquitous in Baroque music, are played with a stress on the dissonance and then relaxing dynamically to the consonance.

These are simple examples of the kind of analysis needed in the creation of one's own interpretation, and embody principles that may be applied throughout.

There are similar melodic fragments skillfully woven into all passages of this kind—hearing them as one plays helps to transform busy texture into smooth melodic lines. Here are some examples:

B-Minor Allemanda:

A-Minor Grave:

D-Minor Allemanda

The monophonic style of composition of the opening bar disguises an important element of its basic harmonic structure that is usually overlooked. When one hears the chordal progression correctly, the following becomes apparent: the first chord—D-minor, root position—lasts until the seventh 16th-note, whereupon it becomes a 6/3. The B-flat is not part of the initial harmony: it's an anticipation of the new chord; however, the scale is usually played as though the whole chord was a 6/3. The following harmonic analyses demonstrate the correct way of understanding the opening gesture:

Perception of this kind is essential. For further discussion as well as fingering suggestions, see chapter 10, "The Lyrical Movements."

Here is another example in which two skeletal melodic lines are extracted from the monophonic texture of another episode:

Notice how the principle melodic thread—the inner voice—runs smoothly through the arpeggiated texture, and that the next note in the sequence doesn't always coincide with the change of harmony but is slightly delayed.

One often hears a slur added to the figure on the last quarter-note of the third measure, as though Bach had omitted it accidentally. The harmonic structure argues against this presumption: even though its figuration is identical to the subsequent groups of four 16th-notes, the fourth quarter is a weak beat. Slurring from the following downbeat figure serves to emphasize its importance as the true beginning of the sequence.

CHAPTER FOUR

The Improvisatory Movements

In general, movements labeled "Adagio" in Baroque repertoire are an invitation to the performer to play with free expression, reacting to the various rhetorical stimuli in the music in a fluid, flexible way, unconstrained by considerations of metronomic precision, so that what results is as natural as speech. The two movements that I categorize as "improvisatory," then, are, in my perception, written-out improvisations, highly ornamented examples of Bach's skill at incorporating different stylistic elements into his compositions and blending them to produce a homogeneous whole.[1] The German aesthetic concept of polyphony on a single stringed instrument pervades this set of six compositions; however, in these movements one also finds exquisite examples of spontaneous-sounding Italianate ornamentation interspersed with subtle and delicate French embellishment. The two improvisatory pieces have an irregular organization similar to blank verse, and beside the application of dynamics, there is a need for speech-like punctuation such as I indicate in the ensuing examples if the melodic line is to be logical and comprehensible. All kinds of punctuation, including silence, are suggested by the harmonic and melodic structure, and both movements provide the performer with ample opportunity for the use of *rubato*, an essential rhetorically expressive device in Baroque music.[2]

---

1. In my opinion, whereas Baroque composers, because of the limitation of our notational conventions, had no choice but to write out their ornamental gestures with mathematical precision, slavish reproduction of the note values was not their intention, but neither should rhythmic flexibility be exaggerated to the point of distortion but subtly applied to avoid unnatural stiffness.

2. This kind of reaction to the various stimuli woven into the musical fabric—accelerating, slowing down, hesitating, none of which were indicated verbally or symbolically—was already advocated by Frescobaldi in his *Toccate e Partite d'intavolatura di cembalo . . . libro primo* (Rome, 1615).

G-Minor Sonata: Adagio

An interesting feature of the descending scale in the opening gesture is the final pair of sixty-fourth-notes, a device Bach frequently used in similar passages. In this case, as a descending third they act as a fork in the vocal road, the B-flat leading upward to the C in the following chord and the G pointing downward toward the F-sharp. This helps us in the organization of the scale, for we can then be thinking of its C as a pivotal point and subtly shape the scale:

In the second measure, we encounter the slurring notation that I mentioned in chapter 1, which is different from common practice today in that a slur would begin from the second of a pair of tied notes, not the first. This particular slur, then, should be read as beginning from the tied C, not the D: this is generally misinterpreted for the sake of comfort, but changing bow direction after the tie spoils the effect of the elaborate 7–8 progression:

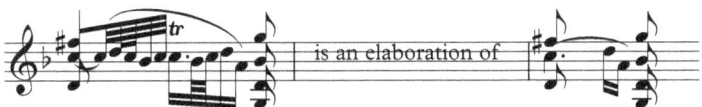

In m. 3, the chord on the third beat, which is traditionally played with an E-flat as the bass note, probably because of the subsequent E-flats in the measure, has become the center of a controversy: did Bach accidentally omit the accidental, or is the notation deliberate? I confess that whereas I recorded the chord in the familiar way, I have come to regret having done so, and now believe that Bach's notation was intentional. One piece of supporting evidence is the fact that Anna Magdalena, in her copy of the work, also wrote the chord without the flat.

Excerpt from the Adagio of the Sonata in G-moll of Bach's "Sei Solo a Violino senza Basso," Mus. ms. Bach P 967, fol. 2r. *Courtesy of Staatsbibliothek zu Berlin—Preußischer Kulturbesitz, Musikabteilung mit Mendelssohn-Archiv.*

A possible explanation is that Bach was simply mirroring the bass-line progression in m. 1. D to E-natural is much stronger than D to E-flat, and, from the rhetorical point of view, hesitating before the pickup notes, then stressing the chord gives a kind of emphasis that leads very effectively toward the chord on the dominant. This is guesswork on my part, but the more I think about it, the more I believe that this was the case. Whatever the truth, there is so much ambiguity in Bach's music that when one chooses between two possibilities, it is most important to rationalize one's choice and to be convinced of one's decision.

Bach makes frequent use of motivic fragments, a reflection of seventeenth-century compositional practice, and the two eighth-note figure at the end of m. 2 occurs in various guises throughout the movement. One generally hears the first similar figure in m. 4 connected by a *Nachschlag* to the previous trilled note:

I disagree with this interpretation. To begin with, the principal voice at the moment is the alto: the soprano is only descant. The downbeat appoggiatura and its briefly trilled resolution, the continuation of the soprano line from the preceding G, are a characteristically French cadential ornament that has no *Nachschlag*, and I perceive this as an interrupted cadence, with the following figure the beginning of the next phrase unit. Besides, if Bach had intended there to be a *Nachschlag*, he would surely have written it.

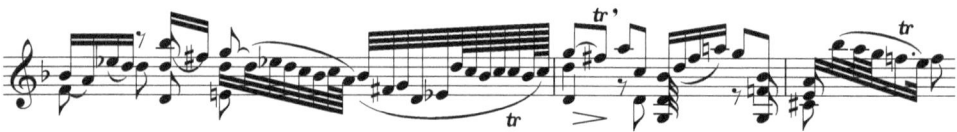

Here is a sample of the kind of nuance and punctuation suggested by the harmonic progressions and melodic contours of the remainder of the first section of the Adagio, and an explanation of my successive choices:

1. The passage begins with a classic 7–6 progression, a pattern that should always be played with a diminuendo.
2. Even though the melodic line is descending through paired sixteenth-notes to the bar line, the addition of the second voice and the harmonic progression to the strong dissonance on the downbeat suggest a rapid crescendo, and the angular spelling of the dissonance has a questioning nature. As with the C in m. 19, the G should be heard here as the continuing bass note.
3. The descending bass line and the 7–6 and 4–3 progressions cause a gradual relaxation of harmonic tension to the downbeat of the next measure.
4. Another 7–6 progression and the intensification of the E by the burst of thirty-second notes lead to the downbeat 7/4–3 dissonance, a slightly questioning pivotal point in the passage.
5. The Lombardic accent and 4–3 progression prepare the approach to the leisurely V–I cadence that ends the section.
6. The commas suggest articulations of varied length, from barely audible *Luftpausen* to rhetorical silences that serve to emphasize the questions that precede them and enhance their effectiveness.

This is the type of analysis to use in order to arrive at a Baroque-style interpretation. Needless to say, it should eventually happen spontaneously, but the choices I have made are based on principles that are simple to adopt.

In m. 7, I use a fingering that preserves the darker color of the melodic line, by starting the fourth-quarter E on the A-string, then blending imperceptibly with the open E in anticipation of the ornamental flourish, and returning to the original color.

Here are some subtleties of interpretation that may not be in accord with traditional interpretation. In the following passage, the rising eighth-note line, appears to suggest a gradual crescendo:

On the other hand, if one takes the harmonic progression into account, it will be treated differently:

The variable appoggiatura should be sustained long enough to enjoy the flavor of the seventh.

In m. 13, I recommend that the slurs, which are somewhat ambiguous in the autograph, be read as follows:

A slight placement of the downbeat serves to establish the C as the first note of the new phrase—effectively a *da capo*—not the completion of a cadence.

The tumultuous climax of the movement (mm. 17–20) calls for dramatic bow strokes. In m. 17, I believe that the F should be played with a separate stroke in order for it to stand out melodically. The rhetorical silences in mm. 18 and 20 allow time to retake the bow.

Rather than leaping to third position to play the trilled F, which would interrupt and spoil the soprano tone color, it is better to stay in first position.

The *Nachschlag* will require an extended fingering despite the awkwardness of the string-crossing, but as a result, the bow will be moving in the direction of the G-string to initiate the chord:

One frequently hears an exaggerated ritardando made in the penultimate measure of the Adagio, with the result that the final ornamental flourish is effectively transformed into a melodic line. This is both unnecessary and un-Baroque. Players who do this overlook the fact that the A in the dominant chord does not resolve immediately to the B-flat, but to the one in the final chord of the movement. The melisma is merely an elaborate way of connecting dominant to tonic as might normally be improvised by the performer, and itself creates, in effect, an allargando:

A-Minor Sonata: Grave

When interpreting a Baroque movement, the first determination to be made is its emotional character or "affect." There are a number of hints incorporated in the music: key, metre, harmonic structure, rhythm, and "the word in the top left-hand corner." *Grave*, as the word suggests, connotes a rather heavy, serious affect, and the bass line's stately quarter-note motion, diatonically descending a fifth before returning chromatically to the dominant, serves to underscore that emotional message.

In order to project the movement's affect, then, pay attention to the strength and regularity of the bass line, yet at the same time seek to play the ornamented melody in a spontaneous-sounding way. There is much less opportunity for the kind of freedom that is the essence of the G-minor Adagio: indeed, most of the movement does not lend itself to the use of *rubato*, but rather "agogic" accentuation—the subtle lengthening of certain notes for emphasis—in order to impart a speech-like feeling.

Whereas the opening notes seem to suggest soprano primacy, I suggest the following alternative reading:

In order to bring out the initial C as melodic, roll the chord up to a double-stopped C and E, releasing the E and prolonging and swelling the C before continuing. Thus, the descent from the first F may be perceived as a graceful ornamental approach to the trilled B, and the melodic contour, instead of giving the impression of repeating the F, focuses attention on the downbeat of m. 2 as the high point of the phrase unit. At the end of m. 2, subtly inflect so that the bass G-sharp acts as a pickup to the next phrase unit, and not the unbroken continuation of the line.

Here is a detailed interpretation of the first section of the movement with suggested nuances and fingerings. Note that it is preferable in scalar passages to play fourth-finger Es and As when ascending and open when descending, because the use of the open string ascending results in too abrupt a change of tone color, whereas it is unnoticeable in the descent. This is, however, not necessary or even desirable in the case of arpeggiated chords, such as in m. 3:

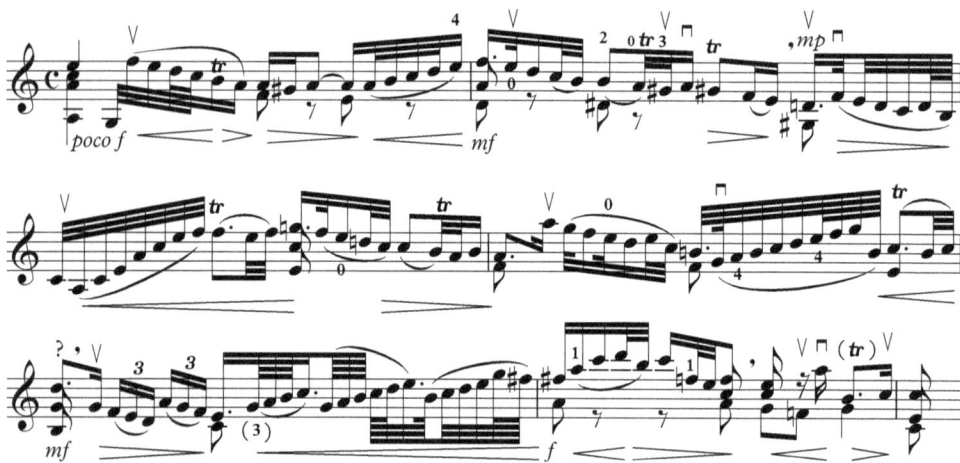

Here again, in m. 6, roll the triads in such a way that the soprano emerges as the sole melodic voice.

Whereas one generally begins a trill on the upper note in eighteenth-century music, I prefer to approach the trill in m. 4 from beneath, slurring to the D instead of leaping to it and thereby emphasizing it. This is a valid alternative:

Note that the appoggiaturas should be placed on the beat, not before.

In m. 7, the best fingering causes the bow to be moving toward the G-string; at the same time, this avoids having to jump sideways with the first finger. Remember that the bass note of any chord must be on the beat. It does not matter that the melodic voice is heard slightly later: arpeggiating chords is a normal Baroque practice.

Descending figures in the following example, such as the one on the first downbeat, and the four sixteenth-notes on the following downbeat, are characteristic cadential gestures in Bach's language, signaling a momentary punctuation of the melodic line:

A word about cadential trills: in three places in this movement, mm. 6, 11, and 21, it is customary to play an upper-note trill on the penultimate dotted eighth-note, even though none is notated: as an example, I have suggested one in example 4.15.[3]

As we see throughout the manuscript, Bach frequently drew his slurs carelessly, but in m. 10, he went to extraordinary trouble to complete the slur in the ascending scale:

Excerpt from the Grave of the Sonata in A-moll of Bach's "Sei Solo a Violino senza Basso," Mus. ms. Bach P 967, fol. 8r. *Courtesy of Staatsbibliothek zu Berlin—Preußischer Kulturbesitz, Musikabteilung mit Mendelssohn-Archiv.*

Here, you can see clearly his intention:

Excerpt from the Grave of the Sonata in A-moll of Bach's "Sei Solo a Violino senza Basso," Mus. ms. Bach P 967, fol. 8r. *Courtesy of Staatsbibliothek zu Berlin—Preußischer Kulturbesitz, Musikabteilung mit Mendelssohn-Archiv.*

3. For other examples of unnotated ornaments, see Leopold Mozart, *Versuch einer gründlichen Violinschule* (Augsburg, 1756), trans. Editha Knocker (London: Oxford University Press, 1948), chapter 11.

However, one often hears the slur broken deliberately, thereby stressing the C-natural, creating a false accent, and changing the meaning of the phrase:

I believe that Leopold Mozart's explanation of the slur—that the first note is the strongest and each subsequent note weaker—is pertinent in Bach's music. What happens here, then, may be perceived as a transposition of the C-sharp, which then falls to the C-natural in a graceful diminuendo. Thereafter, the melodic line continues to grow as far as the diminished-fifth at E, and the phrase ends at m. 12 with a classic IV–V–I cadence:

As he does in the G-minor Adagio, Bach reintroduces the initial bassline progression in m. 14, transposed to the dominant. Notice how elaborate and declamatory this version is, a much more passionate rendition, as suggested by the swirling melismata and the angularity of the passage, whose gradual denouement following the V–I cadence in m. 16 is interrupted briefly by the anguished half-cadence on the diminished-seventh chord in m. 20 before falling finally to the codetta that serves as a bridge to the Fuga (*facing*).

I have incorporated bowings and dynamics in this selection not only because the precise length of several slurs in the facsimile is unclear or ambiguous but also as a sample of a Baroque-style resolution of phrasing nuances. There are, in principle, two basic criteria to be satisfied when deciding on bowing direction: the technical and the musical. The former has to do with the physics of right-hand technique and bow design, the latter, more importantly, with contextual demands. In general, of course, it is normal to use a down-bow on stressed notes and an up-bow on weak ones, just as a crescendo will usually be played up-bow and a diminuendo down-bow. But this will not always be possible. In reading between the lines and endeavoring to interpret the autograph in mm. 17 and 18, I have chosen bowings that arrive down-bow on the downbeat, for it would be unnatural to bow the long/short gestures in m. 20 in reverse.

The Improvisatory Movements

A simple but cardinal principle to be observed when working out the scheme of bowings of a passage is that *bow speed determines nuance*. There is a tendency among modern violinists to use as much bow as possible at all times, no doubt due to pedagogical methods that emphasize the need to project above orchestral accompaniment. This encourages the breaking up of long slurs such as the one in the penultimate measure. However, as I have said elsewhere, one should bear in mind that slurs in Baroque music are not bowing indications but deliberately chosen articulations, and that Bach was a violinist. The length of slurs, therefore, and careful bow division determine the dynamic level, nuances, and shape of a phrase. In the case of the codetta, play the melisma on F, coming after the diminuendo from the soft final cadence, gently in one bow: it is not a melodic fragment but an improvisatory gesture on one harmony that subtly delays the chromatic ascent to the dominant E octave.

I disagree with the customary interpretation of the chromatic sixths, whereby the dynamic fades away to the end of the octave E. Inasmuch as the codetta is a transitional passage whose function is a scene-changing device, preparing the listener for the affect of the Fuga, it seems inappropriate to defeat its purpose in this way. Such an interpretation may be quite effective in Romantic music but seems to be at odds with the Baroque aesthetic. The chromatic line rising to the dominant creates a natural intensification, and I believe that Bach's curious notation, which exaggerates that effect, is intended to anticipate the excitement of the following movement.

The wavy line over the sixths is a device also used by Bach in the Fifth Brandenburg Concerto in both the flute and violin parts during the gradual approach to the harpsichord cadenza. It is possibly an indication of vibrato, but the ominous character of the rising harmonies also suggests a crescendo. Another use of that symbol in eighteenth- and nineteenth-century violin music is actually an indication of right-hand vibrato, a pulsation not dissimilar to *tremolo* in seventeenth-century Italian compositions. I believe, therefore, that in using this device, compounded by the trill on the penultimate D-sharp, Bach was building tension in anticipation of the energetic affect of the Fuga. I do not, therefore, allow the intensity of the dominant to flag, nor do I believe that it's necessary to sustain the whole-note for its full written value: hold it as long as comfortable, then connect without hesitation to the opening pickup measure of the Fuga.

CHAPTER FIVE

The Fugues

One may liken a fugue to an oration, in that the subject is announced simply and is then expounded upon and the subject matter examined in detail and developed. In working through the argument, the orator will reinforce points using various rhetorical devices, all of which have counterparts in musical figures.[1]

In forms of such complexity and magnitude, it is essential to be aware of the architecture of the movement and to understand its structural elements, changes of affect, and dynamic gradations. The fugues epitomize the German musical aesthetic concept of polyphony on a single stringed instrument, and so one must always think of the music horizontally, taking care to bring out the individual melodic lines. Chords are only to be thought of vertically when considering their harmonic function; essentially, though, they are vocal coincidences, points at which two, three, or four voices come together briefly.

The three fugues are an interesting study in affective contrast, reflected in the choice of metre. The G-minor's *alla breve* time signature, coupled with the word *allegro*, suggests a brisk, light affect, tempered by the subject's gently falling direction; the A-minor's rising, leaping eighth-note subject suggests an excited, energetic approach; the C-major's theme, on the other hand—once more an *alla breve*, but this time in note values twice as long—radiates calm optimism.

G-Minor

I find that the principal subject works well bowed "as it comes" throughout the movement, whether starting up- or down-bow. The opening statement can be played this way until the arrival of the first episode, where it will be necessary to take the second sixteenth-note up-bow. The purpose of this is twofold:

---

1. I recommend Judy Tarling's excellent, exhaustive examination of this subject in *The Weapons of Rhetoric* (St. Albans, UK: Corda Music Publications, 2013).

(a) Playing the two sixteenth-notes in the subject (or the two eighth-notes) with consecutive up-bows energizes them, draws attention to them, and tends to equalize them dynamically, whereas the second of each pair should be lighter:

The motivic rhythmic figure is another baroque cliché that appears countless times in eighteenth-century music. For the sake of elegance, as well as the lightness of affect suggested by the time signature and the qualifying word, *allegro*, it is important to avoid accentuating the fourth quarter-note, organizing the subject in this way:

(b) In this way, Bach's varied harmonization is better served:

Without hesitating at the end of the Adagio, start the fugue quietly in the upper third of the bow, using a lifted détaché stroke: the fourth eighth-note will be lengthened to connect to the sixteenth-notes. Use more bow on the second and third beats of m. 2 so as to arrive in the lower half, for unplayable features and passages that would be comfortable on an organ involve compromise on the violin. For example, the following passage includes two instances of the need to sustain a note on one string while simultaneously playing separate notes on the adjacent string but articulated as in the initial statement of the subject:

This can be done without resorting to *portato*, only using pressure of the index finger to articulate the moving notes. Once again, bowing "as it comes" brings one to a down-bow on the tied notes: take care to pace the bow-stroke on the tie so as to leave more room for expression on the dissonance.

Chords should generally be played as they come, and although it is usually desirable for the stronger of a consecutive pair to be played down-bow, it is often necessary, for the character of the fugal subject, to play strong chords up-bow:

The essential challenge in such complex chordal writing is to think horizontally and bring out the individual melodic lines. For a detailed discussion of the appropriate techniques, I refer you to chapter 11 in which I give an exhaustive explanation. However, before applying specific techniques, one should have a clear understanding of the hierarchy of the individual voices, how they interact, and the duration of each gesture.

Here, for example, is an analysis of the motivic structure of the above passage, omitting accompanying voices:

Note how the irregular length and overlapping of the gestures serve first to increase and then to release the tension: in terms of quarter-note "beats" 4 + 5 + 2 + 2 + 3 = 16. The harmonies Bach uses launch this passage strongly, and the reiterated eighth-note triads increase the tension until the climax at the V–I cadence. For the remainder of the passage, the tension gradually decreases, and what happens in the third and fourth measures is a typically conversational exchange, with the first gesture stronger, the second weaker but slightly questioning, and the final gesture almost resigned.

In the following passage, Bach uses a conventional notation of the period (used frequently by Vivaldi, and by Corelli in his Op. 5 sonatas) to indicate some kind of arpeggiation, the choice left to the performer:

My own choices are based on the concept of a lyrical execution that provides a gradual transition from a rolling *bariolage*:

through a slurred pattern that brings out the parallel melodic lines while de-emphasizing the pedal D:

and leading finally to the episode in détaché sixteenth-notes. This is not the only solution, but any type of arpeggiation that starts on the pedal D draws attention to that note and is more rhythmic than lyrical.

The episodes in this fugue are improvisations on a series of harmonies, and their correct organization depends upon awareness of the duration of each harmony. Melodic fragments are woven into the texture: hearing these will also help with organization. It is essential to shape episodic passages as one plays, recognizing the harmonic hierarchy and focusing on principal melodic notes. Needless to say, such information should be incorporated subtly into the texture: failure to do so results in the episode sounding like a technical exercise. I draw your attention to the analytical methods demonstrated in chapter 3.

A-Minor

The subject of this fugue contrasts sharply with the other two: its upward direction and leaping thirds suggest strength and excitement. In order to give the leaping eighth-notes their appropriate character, use a lifted stroke in the lower half of the bow.

The opening three-note gesture is of the nature of a clarion call: its function changes throughout the movement, sometimes as an upbeat, sometimes an interrogatory suffix, but always starting up-bow on the fourth:

Observe that in order to give liveliness and lightness to the sixteenth- and eighth-note figures in the subject, the first note of the clarion call and the down-bows of the leaping pairs (within the crescendo through the bar) should always be stronger than the subsequent ones:

The descending four-note chromatic figure is notated in quarter-notes throughout the movement. As often happens, it is impossible to play these the way they are notated; it is possible, however, to give the impression of sustaining by moving legato from each of them to the following note on the adjacent string:

Note, however, that later in the movement, when they move upward (mm. 148–152), they are written as eighths followed by rests, and the difference is significant:

Here, the eighths in the melodic voice are diatonic and should therefore be played legato while the chromatic notes are released quickly: at this point in the movement, the melody is lyrical, leading to the unique passage in sixths. This passage provides a useful example of Baroque-style nuances and dynamics. The rising sequence suggests a terraced crescendo until the first set of consecutive sixths and then a gradual terraced diminuendo to the sixteenth-note figure, followed by a swell to the cadence:

In the coda, Bach uses these figures in descending and ascending quarter-notes consecutively—an affective alternation, perhaps, of resignation and hope:

The chord on the downbeat of m. 55 of the facsimile is controversial because of what appears to be a heavily drawn E on the bottom line of the staff:

Excerpt from the A-moll Fuga of Bach's "Sei Solo a Violino senza Basso," Mus. ms. Bach P 967, fol. 8v. *Courtesy of Staatsbibliothek zu Berlin—Preußischer Kulturbesitz, Musikabteilung mit Mendelssohn-Archiv.*

In modern editions, this is resolved by the choice of E-B-E as the chord, a simple transposition of its counterpart in the previous unit. I have a different solution: I believe that the correct chord is the 6/3, G-B-E, for the following reasons:

(a) The chord cannot be E-G-B-E because Bach never wrote two notes on the same stem, and there is no separate flag for the G.
(b) The thickness of the stem and sixteenth-note flags strongly suggests that the oversized E is simply an inkblot caused by a drop falling from Bach's quill, through which he drew his pen.
(c) In Anna Magdalena Bach's copy, the chord is given as G-B-E.

Quite apart from these points, it seems to me that the use of the 6/3 chord is musically more satisfactory—a simple "cloning" is weaker, and lacks the harmonic tension that the 6/3 provides.

One of the dynamic indicators to take into account is the tessitura of the voices. In contrasting passages such as mm. 87–94, the subject matter in the alto and soprano voices may be played quite delicately, then, immediately following, when it descends to the lowest register and is harmonized with full chords, very strongly:

In the passage that begins in m. 124, sustain the chromatic quarter-notes while the second eighth-note of each slurred pair is released. Here are some suggestions:

The double-stops in mm. 128–130 require an awkward extension—it is best to advance the thumb and pivot around it, returning in m. 130.

The pairs of slurred sixteenth- and eighth-notes between mm. 166 and 200 should be "tossed off," slightly separating them from each other. If one applies the rule about the slur meaning a diminuendo to all of those in this episode—twos, threes, and fives—a joyous, playful affect results.

In m. 228, Bach has written one of those quick, imprecise slurs that can be read in a number of ways, so an artistic decision must be made. Here are the options, either of the first two of which is valid:

Such decisions are an important part of the editorial process. It is frequently necessary to decide because of context whether Bach has inadvertently omitted a slur, and one has to rationalize, trying to "get into the head" of the composer. An instance of this occurs in m. 30 of the D-minor Allemanda, where there appears to be a slur missing from the last group of sixteenth-notes, but adding one weakens the following downbeat. Here, on the downbeat of m. 206, a similar figure, a sequence begins, and it is hard to understand why there's no slur over the first three 16ths when each of the following units has one. It's normal for the sequential pattern to be established immediately, so I believe that in this case one may assume that there's an error.

The brief coda, with its *stretto* telescoping of the subject, has fragments of the rising chromatic gesture buried in the texture, and a quick diminuendo followed by a two-measure crescendo propels the music to the brilliant melismatic thirty-second-note passage (which ought never to be slurred) and the triumphal final cadence:

C-Major

The subject of this fugue, nobly serene in contrast to the other two, is basically a descending tetrachord, which gives a slightly melancholy cast to the movement despite the normally optimistic C-major affect:

The affect is reinforced by the introduction of a descending chromatic countersubject:

A common misapprehension is that moving notes under ties should be slurred, and the two measures that follow provide a good example of this potential pitfall:

Which should be played thus:

As in the G-minor Fuga, most of the movement may be bowed as it comes, with only occasional retaken down-bows or extra up-bows for phrasing reasons:

In the following example, the bowing of consecutive chords reflects their relative harmonic strength:

A slight placement and prolongation of the F-sharp prepares the final cadential gesture that launches the exuberant episode that follows:

A predominant feature of each of the three episodes is the jagged intervallic motif. In such a passage, it is important to avoid equalization of the eighth-notes but to play the down-bow notes more strongly. To do so, use a slightly lifted stroke, a détaché played just above the middle of the bow, balancing it with the fourth finger: it helps to think of each pair of eighths, down-up, as constituting a single bow stroke. Above all, do not use *martelé*.

I think it's better not to read the last three eighth-notes in each measure as pickups, but rather as the end of a harmonic gesture. That way the energy is focused on each downbeat, whereas playing the eighths as a pickup would weaken it. However, if there were a change of harmony at that point, their function would be quite different.

Whenever possible, choose a fingering that maintains the tone color of each fugal voice. Left-hand technique must frequently be convoluted in order for the voices to flow as smoothly as possible; this passage also demonstrates typical contracted chordal fingerings:

Starting down-bow on the pickup to m. 93 works very well for this extended fugal passage, bowing thereafter as it comes; it is only in m. 98 that it will be more comfortable to take an extra up-bow on the final eighth-note. Note that it is not desirable to slur pairs of eighth- or quarter-notes but rather to play them separately in order to preserve the articulation of the subject and countersubject throughout. It is only when thematic eighths occur under a tie, as in mm. 96, 116, 118, 119, and 120, that it is better to take them in the same direction.

Each of the two extended pedal-tone sections should be played with a smooth détaché, falling away at the beginning of the ascending sequence in preparation for an effective terraced crescendo to the triumphal crowning octave. It's important, though, to stress the melodic down-bows and underplay the repeated notes: inequality of this kind draws attention to the melody and keeps the pedal in the background. Take full advantage of the dynamics suggested by the turbulent sequential structure of the episode (mm. 164–186) to create mounting anticipatory excitement.

The *al riverso* section begins very quietly, subdued after the exultant affect of the preceding passage, but once again the contours of the passage suggest its dynamic structure, a series of fugal entries that reaches a climax fairly early, in m. 217. The preponderance of descending melodic figures thereafter tends to give it a somewhat melancholy character. This is balanced, however, by the optimism of the ensuing episode, which escalates sequentially to sixth position, growing in dynamic to the climactic moment of the movement, before cascading down to the second pedal section. One sometimes hears the climax approached with a diminuendo and played softly: to me, that seems quite anticlimactic, and to make no sense whatsoever in terms of Baroque language. To explain this, imagine, if you will, a sustained pedal-tone, G above middle C, starting in m. 250 and continuing until m. 271, where it would drop an octave to prepare for the following passage. The tension created by the sequences rising and falling against that note dictates a parallel rise and fall of dynamics.

Because of the immediate qualifying harmonization, the *da capo* that follows the second pedal passage is a now-confident reiteration of the opening subject that warrants a relatively strong dynamic level. In rhetorical terms, one might think of this reprise as the summation and proof of the argument. The final chord of the movement, which springs from the passionate exuberance of the final affect, is best played in such a way as to emphasize the C as the final melodic note, with the G in the role of descant.

CHAPTER SIX

The Ostinato Movements

The term *ostinato*, which translates literally as "stubborn," is associated mainly with ground basses, but may be applied also to the persistent repetition of a rhythmic figure or a harmonic pattern, or even, as in the case of Ravel's *Bolero*, to an entire sixteen-measure unit. Two of the most familiar ostinato forms, the Chaconne and the Passacaglia, were interchangeable and even combined or alternated in one composition, which is what Bach chose to do in his monumental Ciaccona.

The Chaconne[1] had its origins in the New World in the late sixteenth century as a song and dance of the lower classes whose irreverent lyrics and vulgar gestures caused it to be condemned by the clergy as the work of the devil. However, soon after its importation into Spain, it became established as a familiar form whose repetitious character and long-winded texts invited its evolution into a vehicle for instrumental variation that seventeenth-century Italian composers were also quick to adopt. Instrumental works such as Frescobaldi's *Partite sopra Ciaccona* (1627) and his *Cento partite sopra passacaglie* (1637), and vocal compositions by others such as Monteverdi and Storace, attest to the recognition of the *ostinato* as a standard musical form. A century later, when Bach composed his Chaconne, the form had evolved from its popular dance-like beginnings into a sophisticated art form whose development had been subject to various national influences. It is interesting to note that Bach composed only two ground-bass works, the C-minor *Passacaglia* for organ (BWV 582) and the *Ciaccona*, both of them monumental in scope. Whereas the latter is unique in Bach's oeuvre and unquestionably a magnificent piece of music, it owes much of its extensive compositional style to French models, notably those of François Couperin, and its tripartite form is similar to that of Heinrich von Biber's *Passacaglia* for solo violin, which predated Bach's composition by approximately forty years.

---

1. I recommend the exhaustive article on *Chaconne* by Alexander Silbiger in *Grove Music Online*.

Partita II: Ciaccona

It is of paramount importance when performing the extended movements in these works—the three fugues and the Chaconne—to be fully aware of their architecture. Without benefit of careful study of the form and structure of such pieces, they are likely to come across as unshapely and illogical. The analysis that follows is offered as an example of the kind of preparation that can lead to a coherent interpretation.

As frequently happens in works of this kind, both forms—Chaconne and Passacaglia—occur in the Ciaccona. They differ from each other in one key respect: the placement of the downbeat accent. The traditional Romantic-style interpretation fails to take into account the fact that the Chaconne starts with a pickup, whereas the Passacaglia, whose bass line is a descending tetrachord, has none. Thus, the tonic triad, which serves as an upbeat in the Chaconne, becomes the downbeat of the Passacaglia:[2]

It is normal to "overdot" in Baroque music, an unnotated rhythmic convention, and the opening statement needs this treatment in order to connect seamlessly to the first variation. Not observing this custom results in the dotted quarter-eighth figure being stiff and heavy-sounding instead of naturally flowing. Hence, the following is the desirable effect and the recommended bowing:

In chapter 11 I devote some time to discussing certain undesirable ways of playing chords in Baroque music. Suffice it here merely to say that one must never begin a chord before the beat or roll it downward: all chords in "unaccompanied" music start on the beat and from the lowest note, for the bass *is* the beat.

One often hears the cadential chord on the downbeat of m. 8 rolled (or, rather, snapped) downward, presumably because the player feels that the final note of the soprano line needs to be placed precisely on the beat, and yet wants to get down as quickly as possible. Each of the succeeding four-note chords is then usually rolled

---

2. It is interesting to note that of the 270 measures that comprise the *Ciaccona*, 121 are Chaconne, and 149 are Passacaglia.

rapidly up and down, the melodic note in the tenor played twice in an attempt to give the impression of lengthening it. The result is a bizarre mixture of the comic and the violent that could hardly be further from the appropriate effect. In order to bring out the tenor line, roll each chord upward starting from a double-stop that favors that voice and making a vertical diminuendo to soften the upper strings.

This involves using more bow at the beginning of the stroke and slowing it down and lightening the bow as you rise through the chord. Here is a bowing that helps preserve the Chaconne's essential dance-like character:

The symbol Z→ indicates the use of "Z-bowing," whereby the arm moves continuously and the sixteenth-note is produced with a reverse flick of the hand. When this technique is used, the effect is a smooth back-and-forth arm motion that avoids the angularity of the hook-stroke, which is a derivative of *martelé*, a nineteenth-century innovation that has no place in Baroque music. The bowing prescribed above is appropriate for the entire passage of dotted eighths and sixteenths. (Obviously, in the measures in which there are thirty-seconds, which should be played with separate strokes, no adjustment of direction is necessary.) Notice the octave shift in the bass line in the third variation, indicating a more delicate dynamic for the remainder of the first section.

Next, having exhausted the possibilities of the dotted rhythm, Bach introduces a descending cantabile motif with a sixteenth-note variation that transforms subtly into the first iteration of the *Passacaglia*. The form of this section begins like that of Biber's—each four-measure unit followed by a more elaborate variation—but he then blurs the distinction between the two by having the second four measures invert the pattern to conclude the eight-measure unit. Observe in this example how the scales in the fifth and seventh measures move in opposite directions to those in the first and third:

The articulations in mm. 50 and 51 are slightly ambiguous in the facsimile, and in some editions, one finds the slur beginning on the second note of the measure. However, I believe that only the seven-note scale should be slurred:

Separating the passage into its component parts, my reasoning is as follows: first, this is a Passacaglia and therefore the downbeat of each measure is strong; to convey that strength, it is most effective to bracket the first two notes of the bar. The scale constitutes one separate, quasi-parenthetical gesture, and its grouping accords with the principle of slurring notes that have something in common. Finally, as the last note of the slur is by definition the weakest, the last three notes of each bar lead into the new downbeat in a syncopated gesture, the D falling to the C, the C to the B-flat, the B-flat to a delayed A.

In this way, of course, the sequential bowing pattern is preserved, which is another persuasive argument. This is the moment in the movement at which Bach gives the first hint of the energy to come, and whereas the transition to the climax of the section is gradual, the warning signs—the octave and sixth leaps—signal a perceptible change from the previous meandering affect. The scales, by contrast, are looking back at that affect, thereby subtly smoothing the transition. The jaggedly arpeggiated sixteenth-notes that follow continue to raise the level of excitement, leading to the declamatory passage that is the climax of the first section of the work.

It is not appropriate to emphasize the sixteenth-notes in mm. 66, 67, and 68, nor in 71, 72, and 73. In these bars, the first beat is strong and the third weak, and the second should be tossed away lightly. Similarly, the three sixteenth-notes in mm. 74 and 75 are often played much too loudly for the context:[3] this has the effect to deemphasizing the following downbeats, which are important melodic notes out of which spring the thirty-second-note scales.[4]

---

3. There are those in the modern violin community who seem to think that the G-string is the greatest invention since the wheel and intentionally play these notes and similar others throughout the entire set of pieces very loudly. This is absolutely un-Baroque, as is forcing the sound of the final note of a section or movement.

4. I don't believe that Bach accidentally omitted a trill on the penultimate sixteenth-note of m. 75, but that its omission is an elegant variation.

In m. 78, after the breathless energy of the thirty-second-notes, it is better not to change affect abruptly, as is often the custom. Imagine, if you will, that after all of the exertion of the passage, you're out of breath, your heart rate is rapid, and that it will take a while for it to return to normal. So, use the next eight measures to come gradually down to a quieter affect.

There is a magical quasi-Impressionist quality to the arpeggiated section—try to create a luminous, translucent tone color and allow the passage to bloom to a gentle *forte* at its peak, never forcing the sound: the climax of the first section of the movement is past, and it is unfortunate and unnecessary to rival its intensity.

Focus your attention throughout on the moving voices: in sections such as the following, it is very easy to emphasize the outer parts and neglect the inner, so careful balance is essential:

Here is an exercise that I prescribe to ensure that the inner voice is well balanced. Play each eighth-note well sustained and with full tone:

One often hears a performance in which the arpeggio pattern prescribed by Bach is abandoned and one in triplets and at times a four note pattern substituted. This is quite unnecessary: a virtuoso arpeggiation exercise in Geminiani's treatise gives us a clue as to the way to maintain Bach's version throughout.[5] The exercise is based on a set of chords all except one of which is a triad, the sole exception being a four-note chord that is played each time by simply sounding the bottom two notes as a double-stop. One can use this technique here, which avoids changes to new patterns:

5. Francesco Geminiani, *The Art of Playing on the Violin* (London, 1751).

In order to preserve the melodic flow, relax the repetition of each harmony so that eighth-note pulsations do not predominate:

As the passage descends, it is more effective to allow the dynamic to diminish until the final cadence, and not revive with the arrival of the filigree melismata in m. 124, treating them rather as delicate wisps of sound above a dying final tetrachord. Then, after the cadence on the downbeat of m. 128, one may make a rapid crescendo to the return of the initial material in a more powerful guise that surges to a climax in m. 131 before gradually ebbing away to the end of the first section and the beginning of the *maggiore*.

A certain degree of *rubato* is desirable in some gestures in the coda of the first section. A slight delay and shortening of the separate sixteenth-notes in mm. 124–127 and also of the final eighth-notes in mm. 132–135 gives a more natural, improvisatory flow to the line: playing the rhythm literally results in a stiff, pedantic rendition.

The *maggiore*, the second extended section of the movement, starts again as a Chaconne, simply and quietly, but undergoes a rapid escalation after the initial statement. It gains momentum in the second phrase with a rambling eighth-note line reinforced by the reiteration of the original rhythmic motif. Eight measures later, after a strong cadence, Bach introduces sixteenth-notes as a Passacaglia, at first in a questioning manner, but then in a strongly arpeggiated passage that grows to a climax in m. 161 before falling rapidly away to the beginning of a new motivic sequence. At this point, in m. 162, instead of emphasizing the three-note repetition, it is more effective not to draw attention to it, but rather to introduce it quietly and casually, even treating the subsequent *unisono* version and the first four-note group in a matter-of-fact way. Playing the passage thus, as Bach gradually increases the tension by repetition and expansion of the motif and with cascades of repeated double-stopped intervals, leaves room for a dramatic crescendo to end the section fortissimo.

The next, lyrical phrase is best bowed as it comes, and I incorporate a few fingering suggestions designed to facilitate a cantabile rendition:

The abrupt change of affect signaled by the robust triadic treatment of the material in m. 188 calls for much stronger articulation, so a reiterated down-bow pattern is appropriate until the melodic line begins to rise diatonically, and the triadic texture assumes an intense cantabile character as the phrase moves toward the final cadence and the grand arpeggiated conclusion. Even though it's impracticable to overdot this section to the same degree as in the opening phrase, a slight lengthening of the dotted quarter-notes, playing the eighth-notes slightly later and shorter than written, helps to maintain the flow.

Bach leaves the pattern of the new arpeggio passage to the performer: my own preference is for a rolling thirty-second-note arpeggiation to capture the full-organ magnificence of the moment:

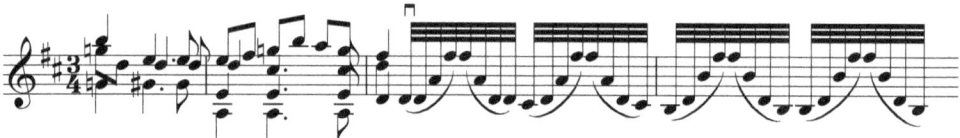

After the triumphal utterance of the *maggiore's* final cadence, the concluding section of the *Ciaccona* begins quietly and almost apologetically, with a series of questioning dissonances for six of the first eight measures. When the Passacaglia returns, though, twelve measures of sixteenth-note improvisation culminate in a burst of energetic thirty-seconds that herald the arrival of the coda. Here is a suggested fingering that leads seamlessly into the coda:

The bow stroke at the beginning of the coda is known as *ondeggiando*, literally "swaying": the bow passes from one string to the next smoothly, with a little overlegato to soften the string-crossing, so that the effect is slightly blurred and the open A understated. The passage begins quietly, and the dynamic level falls away even more during the descending chromatic line, to prepare the way for a gradual return, as the line rises, to *forte* with the rapid triplets and the arching dominant melisma that brings us to the final statement of the Chaconne motif.

In my opinion, the partita ends not in triumph but in repose, as though returning to the affect of the *Allemanda*: although the first four measures of the coda replicate the majesty of the previous statements, there follows a descending bass line that has the effect of deflating their intensity, and, after a poignant melismatic arpeggiation, the two remaining voices come together to fade away in a peaceful unison.

Sonata III: Adagio

The dotted figure that pervades the opening movement of the third sonata qualifies it for inclusion in this chapter as a rhythmic *ostinato*. I believe that there are two principles to observe when playing this movement:

Tactus: "All music is in one"—avoiding beating time in quarter-notes
Rhythmic flexibility: the sixteenth-note given less than its literal value

For me, the first of these is a cardinal rule that relates to metre and harkens back to the earlier practice of *tactus*: it was customary to beat time twice per measure, one down and one up ("arsis" and "thesis"), and the pulse would relate approximately to the normal human heart rate, that is, from seventy to eighty-four beats per minute. The two-beats-per-measure concept was current until the eighteenth century and is one that I find useful when explaining tempo or the flow of a gesture or phrase.[6] As regards tempo, consider the fact that before the advent of the metronome, composers had to rely on symbolic notation to signal their intention,[7] and that the composer's choice of metre in Baroque music frequently served that function.[8] For example, the difference between $\frac{12}{8}$, $\frac{6}{8}$, and $\frac{3}{8}$ when the principle is applied is that the eighth-notes become proportionately slower.

---

6. Mattheson, op. cit.
7. For a comprehensive survey of the subject, see Geoffrey Chew and Richard Rastall's article on "Mensural Notation from 1500" in *Grove Music Online*.
8. There were also, of course, certain regional conventions regarding the tempo of the various dance forms. See chapter 2.

Qualifying indications, such as *allegro, adagio, andante,* and *presto,* already found in the earliest violin compositions, are best thought of in terms of affect, rather than "fast" or "slow." Indeed, the only Italian qualifying word with a literal "tempo" meaning is *lento* (slow).[9] The sense of *adagio* (literally "at ease") is quiet or calm, and to project the tranquil, pensive affect of this movement, observe both of the above-mentioned principles. Observance of the second principle—rhythmic flexibility—is essential in a movement such as this, whose basic motif rendered literally would be stiff and lacking in speech-like spontaneity. Leopold Mozart proposed the use of double-dotting as a normal rendition of the dotted eighth-sixteenth rhythm: I think that this would be too jagged in this context, however, and draw attention to itself, so I prefer a more relaxed version, a gently rocking sextuplet. This is only a rough guideline: what matters most is that the figure sounds completely natural, spontaneous, and unaffected.

In my teaching, I make frequent use of analogy, and in this movement, to impart the sensation of flowing motion, I suggest to my students that they imagine wavelets in a lake. To create the feeling of tactus—of feeling the movement "in one"—imagine them receding gently in each of the first two measures, but then in the third allow the music to rise to a plateau in the fourth. The last note of the fourth measure can have a more melodic function, leading over the bar line to the first peak of the phrase, which then descends briefly to relax in m. 6 before intensifying again to its apex in mm. 9 and 10, and falling away gradually to the cadence in m. 15:

The question of slurs in this movement is a vexing one. Was Bach being deliberate in omitting them in so many measures? Was there an assumption of continuity—a kind of shorthand to save ink? Or was he creating ambiguities to be resolved by the performer? I prefer to believe the latter, for it seems to me that playing identical slurs throughout, especially in the climactic measures, would be predictable and tedious. Besides, adding or withholding slurs according to context leaves room for greater variety of expression. Here are some suggestions (*facing*):

---

9. Once again, I recommend the articles on tempo and *lento* in *Grove Music Online*.

In mm. 34, 35, and 36, we have to make an artistic decision about the articulation, choosing between slurring the eighth-sixteenth-note pairs smoothly or gently articulating them. In either case, the half-note should be sustained, and the articulating done with index-finger pressure only:

In m. 41, I believe that the chord should still be rolled upward, despite the fact that the scale rises from the G.[10] The scales are only elaborate ways to arrive at the principal melodic notes, in this case C, D, and E-flat. Bach's notation of the chord in m. 41 would suggest that the double-stop C/F-sharp should be sustained: perhaps, then, one should focus on the progression of the three dissonant double-stops in this passage, in the third of which the suspended D swells to the descending scale instead of falling away.

In the manuscript, the slur on the scale in m. 40 is broken at the end of the staff, but because of the way the other two are written, and a similar case in the A-minor *Grave*, I feel comfortable in assuming that the slur should be continuous. Similarly with the beams over the scale passages—there seems to me to be no good reason not to make each one continuous. I recognize that my decision to link all three scales in this way is artistic license, and you may wonder why I feel that such a trivial detail is so important. But as I see it, the customary mathematical organization of groups of like notes can have the effect of discouraging a flowing approach: for me, the visual

---

10. See chapter 11, "Right-Hand Technique." Do not break the chord downward.

effect is crucial to the perception of phrasing. I must also confess that having lived with and studied this manuscript for so long, I find that modern printed notation obstructs and obfuscates the poetry of the music, and I apologize to the reader for having to use it in my musical examples. I do, however, urge my students to make the effort to become familiar with Bach's handwriting.

In m. 44, the G and D must be clearly articulated, not legato; the C is tied over until the D sounds, and it then becomes the upper note of a trill. You'll notice that in the examples I have added cadential trills in mm. 11 and 14; I also like to add an upper-note trill on the last chord as the B begins to fade. All of these trills can be brief and fairly slow.

The *Fuga* should begin immediately.

CHAPTER SEVEN

The Dancelike Movements

Bourée and Borea

The Bourée as a social dance was a relatively complex mixture of leaps, hops, and the *tems de courante* (a gesture consisting of a bend, rise, and slide), and Bach's sole movement of this genre in his third Partita clearly transmits the nature of the choreography. The characteristic, light energy of this dance is projected by the use of lifted bow-strokes on the first two quarter-notes and clear articulations thereafter:

One of Bach's stylistic hallmarks is the use of motivic fragments. The five slurred notes in m. 1 create a pattern that recurs at various times throughout the movement, which aids in the clarification of some of the less carefully drawn articulations in the manuscript. In mm. 5–8, I believe that there should be five eighth-notes in the slurred group, analogous to the five slurred notes in the first bar.

However, in mm. 21–25, where Bach's intentions are unclear, the articulations may be read in two ways—either as five or six slurred notes—so an artistic decision must be made. Either choice is valid, but the argument in favor of six is that the bowings are more comfortable violinistically, which is always a consideration.

Each of the echoes in mm. 12 and 24 ends on the seventh note of the measure and the eighth is a strong pickup:

Tempo di Borea

The punctuation of the theme with three- and four-note chords makes this an even stronger version of the Bourée. Indeed, the declamatory verticality of the accentuation suggests a leaping or strutting choreography and, in consequence, a somewhat slower tempo than that of its cousin. Once again, there is a pervading motif, a percussive rhythmic pattern that should be strongly etched in the affect I suggest:

The opening measures contain some chords that require contorted fingering:

In mm. 25–28, there is more unorthodox fingering and another instance of the need for articulated moving notes under a tie:

There are, though, a few lyrical notes to offset the constant athletic energy:

Here is a suggestion for the fingering and bowing of the conclusion of the movement—the Double should begin without hesitation:

Its Double

Note the use of the three eighth-note pickups, a motivic feature of this section of the Borea that replaces the single quarter-note upbeat, whose organizing function should be subtly observed with barely perceptible placement or nuance:

Its occurrence is not always obvious from the notation but linked to the various cadences, and one should be conscious of the harmonic progressions. For example:

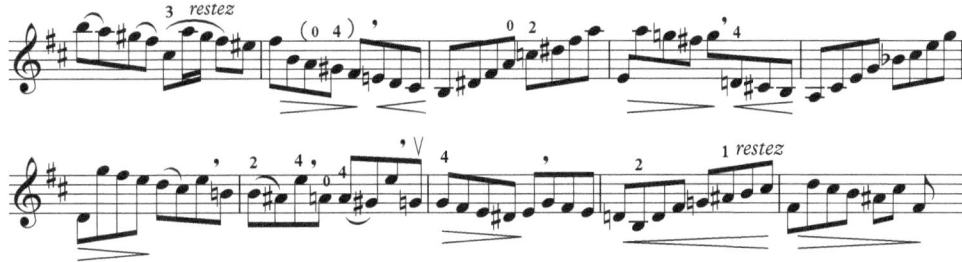

In this and the following example, I have added fingerings that demonstrate the use of half-position to maintain the clarity of sound desirable in music of this kind. In principle, it's better to avoid playing above first position unless absolutely necessary. I have also added typical nuances and dynamics:

B-Minor Corrente

This movement derives its sprightliness from detached arpeggios, ascending and descending, in contrast with and balanced throughout by three-note slurred figures. The ideal tempo, though, is moderate, the bow stroke slightly lifted and somewhat soft-edged in keeping with the characteristic softness of the key. Bach's choice of metre is significant: the alternation of full and half bar-lines organizes the music into what is effectively a slow $^6_4$, a type of *alla breve*:

The barring does not preclude shifts of accentuation in the scansion. In the concluding measures of each section, and also after the double bar, Bach introduces asymmetry:

Bach takes the pair of notes that cross the bar lines at the second and fourth measures and extends them to create a pattern that needs a special fingering in order to reflect voice-leading and preserve tone color. It's best to play each pair of chromatic notes on the same string:

Similar passages that occur in the second section of the movement require similar treatment:

The concluding phrase of the movement contains another passage that must be played in half position, which is so often necessitated by Bach's violin writing:

(The Double is treated in chapter 8, "The Virtuoso Movements.")

D-Minor Corrente

The energy in this rapidly moving Corrente is the product of two musical devices—triplet motion and a strong, recurring rhythmic motif:

This "one-two" accentuation appears in numerous places throughout the movement. For example, in the third measure, it is hidden in the dotted rhythm:

Later, in the "coda," it recurs several times:

For the sake of clarity of voice-leading, it is essential to stay in first position in m. 1: the angular string-crossing from C-sharp to B-flat preserves the vocal tone-color while transmitting a sense of excitement. Sustaining the open A and then the F in the second bar for their full length gives the impression of legato motion between the A and B-flat, and the F and G:

Because of the overall triplet context, the dotted notation in the subsequent measures is better rendered as long-short triplet rhythm, although with the energetic lightness implied by the dotted notation and characteristic of the overall affect:

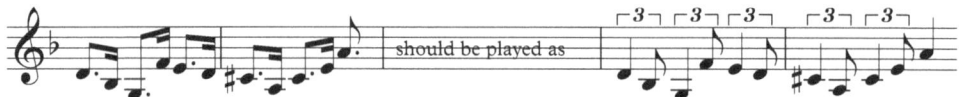

Using "Z-bowing," allow the bow to "travel" from heel to point so as to be ready for the series of long up-bows that follows. This is a technique that I describe in chapter 11, "Right-Hand Technique," and what is demonstrated here may be applied throughout the movement:

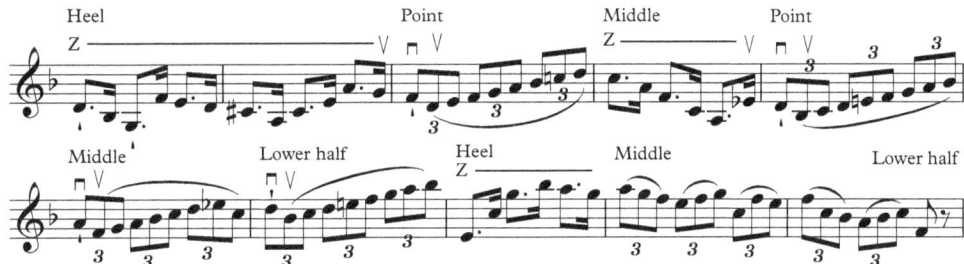

In m. 36, I prefer to read the articulations as short/long, which are more energetic, besides which the bowing works out well:

The articulations in mm. 40 and 41 of the manuscript are not clear, but if one reads them as whole-measure slurs, the result is an escalation of energy that is quite effective:

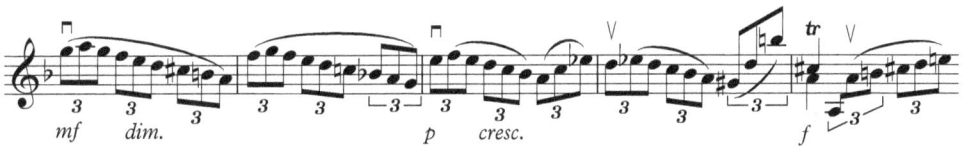

In mm. 49 and 50 the eighth-notes may be played as a kind of melisma that flows without accentuation to the downbeat of m. 51, the next strong impulse, which gives the final phrase a decisive affect:

Stretching the tied quarter-notes slightly makes the motivic emphases even stronger: after the second one, sprint to the finish line without slowing down. I choose to end with a unison in order to amplify the sound with the resonance of the open string.

Gavotte en Rondeau

One often hears a performance of this movement in which an impulse is placed on the upbeat. In the dance, however, the pickup notes are introductory—the first strong step occurs on the downbeat. In any case, from the harmonic point of view, the tonic upbeat is weaker than the two subsequent downbeats, especially given their strong dissonance. To achieve the appropriate weak/strong relationship, then, I prefer to play the upbeat quarter-notes up-bow:

In this example, I have inserted staccato dots to indicate lifted articulations, stresses on the strong harmonies, and commas to separate phrase units. Note that the trill on the seventh should not begin from above but on the note itself so as not to negate the flavor of the dissonance.

The *rondeau* form, characteristic of similar French music, subdivides the movement into nine sections: the initial rondeau occurs (not counting the first repeat) five times, and there are four episodes, the first eight measures long, the second and third each sixteen measures, and the final one twenty. There are two types of affect in the episodes: the first and third are somewhat dark, whereas the second and fourth are optimistic. The first episode begins with a crescendo, even though the bass line is descending, because of the intensification of the harmonies:

The phrasing of the second episode is frequently misunderstood, and one often hears it played like this:

The tendency is to stress the entrance of the second voice; however, Bach's quarter-note rest suggests that the second voice actually enters silently on the downbeat and grows dynamically. The correct reading is:

Placing a slight accent on the next downbeat clarifies the shape of the phrase.

Once again, Bach puts a motivic fragment to use, in this instance the first three quarter-notes of the episode. Focusing attention on the rhythmic energy of the upper voice helps one toss off the moving eighth-notes in the lower voice more lightly:[1]

Always be conscious of the conversational elements in this music, as exemplified in the third episode. When this passage is broken down into its basic units, a dialogue emerges. Let's call the conversing parties A and B:

1. A curious feature of this episode is the inclusion in the manuscript of fingering of the seventh in m. 34. This annotation—remarkably, the only place in the entire volume in which fingering appears—could, of course, be the work of someone other than Bach, and one does wonder why there is none in places that are much more awkward. Be that as it may, if you compare the "3" with any of those in the triplet figures, and the "1" with those in page numbers, you'll notice that the handwriting seems to be identical.

The rondeau that follows, starting as it does with an emphatic 6/3 upbeat, should be played in a way that sets the stage for the final episode, which is unusually dramatic for inclusion in a Gavotte, one of the most elegant of French Baroque dances. It is a veritable cadenza, with declamatory outbursts in a fragmented structure, in a style whose origins are to be found in late-seventeenth-century virtuoso violin music by composers such as Biber, Walther, and Westhoff. Here are suggestions for dynamic shaping, bowings, and phrase organization:

The Giga

In order that this movement be played gracefully and not degenerate into a *moto perpetuo*, a mere exercise in virtuosity, the principle of "All music is in one"—one strong and one weak beat per measure—may be applied. To be sure, there are numerous places where there are quarter-note impulses as well as half-note, but if the sixteenths, which are generally improvisations on the harmonies, flow effortlessly from one impulse to the next, there will be an almost leisurely feeling to the pace of the music.

Be sure to play the downbeat of m. 3 with a strong impulse: the melodic line is misleading, for it looks as though there's a V–I cadence, but the downbeat is actually a 6/3, not a root-position tonic chord, and is the first element of a descending sequence that leads to its final resolution in m. 6.

I choose to finger the echo passages, mm. 11–12 and 27–28, identically despite the frequent use of the fourth finger. I believe that as a general rule sequential or imitative passages are best fingered identically:

Sustaining the finger does help, though:

In mm. 16–17, I prefer to use the open E because of the arpeggiated nature of the gesture. Allow the descending scales to feel relaxed, like an exhalation, and the rising sequential gestures to revive the energy. Here is a suggested reading using the kind of dynamics, nuances, and accentuation applicable throughout the movement:

In the manuscript, there is no slur over the last three eighth-notes in the measure after the double bar, and I believe that this was intentional. An added slur, as one often hears, seems to me to be too predictable, and weakens the C-sharp: when the last two eighths are played separately and lifted, the effect is much livelier:

This may seem like a minor point, but it touches on aesthetic concepts that are central to Baroque performance practice and define some of the basic differences between that and the traditional Romantic-style approach to music of the eighteenth century. These include avoiding predictability, letting less important notes go, playing in a spontaneous and natural way, and never imposing oneself on the music.

The overriding aesthetic concept is that of *affect*, the emotional message of the music: before playing any movement, always ask yourself, "What is the affect?" Naturally, there will usually be more than one answer—different shades of emotion or, in extended movements, contrasting affects—but it is essential to have a particular one in mind at the outset. In creating the most effective interpretation, then, disregard the pedantic view that each movement has a single affect, and be alert to subtle shifts of emotion as suggested by the various devices of rhythm, harmony, and articulation employed by the composer. In the case of the Giga, the rising eighth-note figures, the exuberantly arpeggiated sixteenth-notes, the frequent leaps, the cascading sequences and the scurrying passage work all suggest a positive, excited emotion, and my choice for a basic affect is joy.

The Gigue

Metrically, the Gigue is initially an *alla breve*: that is, whereas the Giga's strong and weak beats occur within each measure, the strong/weak impulses of the Gigue straddle the bar line. However, whereas the movement has an apparently simple thirty-two-measure structure, the first section contains an interesting irregularity: after the initial four-measure phrase, the next twelve are grouped five/three/four. What this means in terms of interpretation is that the regularity of the strong and weak accents is interrupted:

The second section is quite regular in terms of basic structure, the variety resulting from the alternation of two-measure and one-measure units:

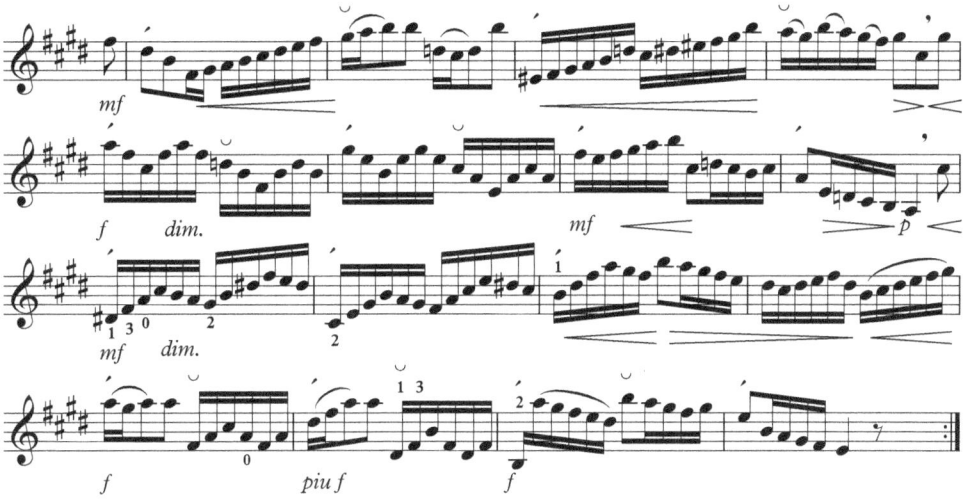

The Loure

The two-note pickup figure that occurs throughout this dance movement has a characteristic lilting quality that epitomizes the concept of rhythmic alteration so common in eighteenth-century music. In order to play this figure correctly, the value of the eighth-note must not be literal but virtually reduced to that of a sixteenth. The gentle character of this *loure* dictates that the dotted rhythm be subtly and elegantly "swung," not crisply snapped. The lightly lilting affect of the piece is thereby established:

One way to understand this is that each dotted quarter-note is shorthand for a quarter tied to an eighth: notice how Bach's notation changes in m. 4 to a dotted eighth and a sixteenth instead of two eighth-notes as soon as the pitch drops on the second quarter. So it is throughout the movement: I believe that there should be no difference between the rhythm of the dotted quarter-note-eighth-note and the quarter-dotted eighth-sixteenth:

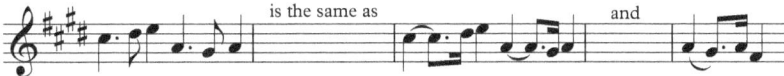

Muffat's description of the bowings used by Lully's orchestra includes the rule that the note following a rest should be played down-bow, which works very well in the pickup figure. In this example, I have used staccato dots to represent a gentle lift of the bow after each quarter-note:

Starting in the lower half, take the bowing as it comes, never resorting to hookstroke, and articulate the third note of each group. I recommend an approximate tempo of quarter-note = 108. As usual, the half-notes in m. 3 and the quarter-note in m. 4 should be shortened so there can be no confusion about which is the principal melodic voice. The dotted motif is to be played as a Z-bowing—in that way, the flowing lyricism of the melodic line and the dance-like elegance of the movement will be preserved:

A contracted fingering is necessary after the double bar and also in the penultimate measure:

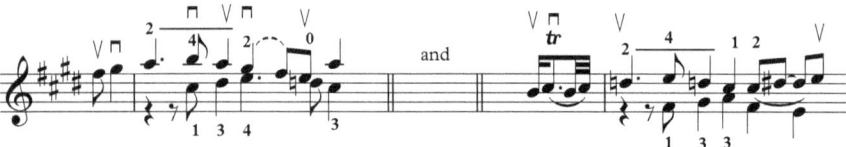

There is, as I see it, a rhythmic conundrum in m. 12: in the fifth quarter-note of the bar, the upper voice has a pair of eighth-notes that should be played equally, while the lower voice has the dotted motivic pattern:

In my opinion, therefore, the two eighth-notes cannot coincide. Using the same pattern of overdotting, the effect will be:

The Menuets

One of the interesting elements of Baroque style and an important feature of the Menuet are *notes inégales*: notes of equal written value performed unequally. Although the practice dates back to the Spanish Renaissance, it is principally associated with eighteenth-century French music and is a feature described in many sources, but, except in extreme versions, it cannot be notated. Its purpose is to facilitate the flow of the music, and it can exist in a variety of forms and degrees. A clear indication of the normalcy of the practice in French Baroque music is that most of the rules given in contemporary sources have to do with when *not* to use them. Those who wish to read about the topic in depth are directed to the article in *Grove Dictionary of Music*.[2]

One of the challenges faced when playing *notes inégales* is that they must sound completely improvisatory. It is therefore desirable to avoid constant identical degrees of inequality, but try to mix and vary. Unfortunately, as with anything unnotatable, it's impossible to convey adequately the sense of inequality in words, so the best advice I can give is to listen to various early music performers and groups playing French music: well done, it's an extremely subtle device; without it, the music sounds wooden and inflexible.

Inequality was normally reserved for the first subdivisions of principal note values: in $\frac{3}{4}$ or $\frac{4}{4}$, therefore, it would be at the eighth-note level, and because Bach was composing in a French style, I believe that it is appropriate to play many of the eighth-notes in these Minuets unequally. There are three ways to do this—long-short, short-long (the so-called "Lombardic" rhythm), and strong-weak. As an example, the eighths in the first bar of Menuet I could be subtly long-short and the slurred pair in the second, short-long. In m. 4, the degree of inequality could gradually decrease through the six eighth-notes, and those in m. 6 could be long-short, long-short, and short-long for variety.

Among the rules cited in contemporary French sources is one that forbids the use of inequality in groups of more than two slurred notes, and so the eighth-notes in the opening Musette-like measures of Menuet II would most probably be played equally. The leaping ones in the fifth bar would be of the strong-weak variety and the slurred ones in the sixth short-long. Regardless of the type of inequality used, the second (up-bow) note should always be played more lightly.

---

2. *Notes inégales* [Fr.: "unequal notes"] "A rhythmic convention according to which certain divisions of the beat move in alternately long and short values, even if they are written equal" (David Fuller, *Grove Music Online*).

These suggestions are a sample of the kind of rendition now taken for granted in performances by "early music" specialists. Needless to say, playing comfortably in French Baroque style requires considerable immersion, for it is without doubt the most esoteric of all. Above all, the effective use of *notes inégales* requires subtlety and a certain degree of nonchalance.[3]

The kind of bow stroke appropriate for the minuet matches the dance step: the name of the dance is derived from *menu*, the French word for tiny, and the bow strokes should be concise and lifted after each quarter-note. The patterns of strokes and the nuances are highly stylized: generally, the third quarter-note of the measure is the lightest: often, playing it with a down-bow, as well as on the following downbeat, will produce that effect better than taking it in an extra up-bow.[4] It is important always to organize the phrasing in two-measure basic units, reflecting the choreography, and combining two units into a four-measure grouping.

The appoggiatura (from the Italian *appoggiare*, to lean upon or support) is the most common Baroque ornament other than the trill. There are two types: variable and invariable. Identically notated, both are played on the beat, but the invariable ones, which have no discernable value or melodic function, are typically used to energize a series of repeated notes or to highlight single ones. Variable appoggiaturas are dissonant, and their function is to delay a consonance gracefully or to emphasize a beat. They can be of any length that seems appropriate to the context and always stronger than the main note. The one in m. 12 is most gracefully rendered as a quarter-note—a half-note would be too languid, and anything shorter too abrupt for the character of the dance. Here is a sample of characteristic bowing patterns and nuances—play in the lower half of the bow:

The pedal tone at the start of the second minuet imitates the drone of a *musette*, a type of bagpipe. Obviously, the note cannot be sustained without changes of bow direction, although it is important to mask these while articulating between the slurs in the melody as if there were no drone. In my own interpretation, therefore, I employ the same technique as when there are separate notes under a tie, in this case incorporating appropriate slurs:

---

3. A familiar modern counterpart is the jazz custom of "swinging" eighth-notes.

4. Your attention is drawn to David Wilson's excellent translation of the preface of Georg Muffat's *Florilegium Secundum* in which the bowing patterns used by Lully's orchestra in the court of Versailles are recorded.

It is customary to finish by playing Menuet I a second time. Regarding repeats, all should be observed with the possible exception, during the *da capo,* of the second section of the first Minuet, which is unusually lengthy.

The Sarabande and Sarabanda

Sarabandes were notated in a variety of rhythmic patterns. In the case of the two movements of this genre in this set of pieces, Bach distinguished them from each other not only by name but in the manner of composition as well—the first in French style, with even quarter-note motion, and the second, Italian, strongly syncopated: the "Sarabande" with a gently lyrical affect, the "Sarabanda" with dramatic energy.

The B-Minor Sarabande

The characteristic accentuation suggested by the choreography is manifested in the first bar of the B-minor Sarabande by the harmonic progression from tonic to subdominant seventh. Only a slight emphasis is necessary, more of the nature of a swell over the measure, taking care not to stress the third quarter but passing over it lightly to the resolution on the downbeat of m. 2.

The $\frac{9}{8}$ metre of the Double suggests to me the subtle use of *notes inégales,* not so regular as to be perceived as triplet eighths but gently swung. They may also be subtly *Lombardic* occasionally, as, perhaps, on the first beat of m. 7 or the second and third beats of m. 21. The purpose of this kind of rhythmic alteration, as in the Menuet, is to enhance the flow of the movement, for equal eighth-notes tend to sound too rigid in such a context. It is not necessary to slur the eighths in mm. 1, 3, or 7.

The figure on the third quarter-note of mm. 5 and 27 is most likely a written-out mordent with all three notes slurred and tossed off lightly in a tempo slightly faster than metronomic:

Its Double

We may assume that the style of a Double reflects the mood of the movement, and conversely, as I have suggested above, can also be a useful indication of the style of the movement itself. An elegant diminution, this Double weaves a tapestry of triplet eighth-notes around the harmonic matrix in a leisurely flowing affect. Since each section is repeated, it lends itself to variation by the addition of slurs. Remember that anything added to the basic text constitutes embellishment, be it dynamics, ornamental notes, or, in this case, articulations.[5] Here is a typical sample:

The general guidelines for the addition of articulations are that they should not complicate the bow direction unnecessarily (the appropriate stroke in this case is a gentle *détaché* just above the middle of the bow), and that the notes slurred should have something in common, such as being an arpeggiated chord, a group of diatonic notes, or neighboring tones. Never slur from one harmony to another. I also encourage my students not to "work out" their variation and write slurs into the music but rather to improvise them spontaneously.

The D-Minor Sarabanda

Whereas in choreographic terms the second beat of the Sarabanda may be accented, we should not assume that this is applicable in the current context. It would be very unnatural in this case to play the double-stop in each measure more strongly than the four-note chord that precedes it. The desired effect can be achieved by rolling the chord quickly down-bow with plenty of lift and the sensation of falling to the double-stop. What is striking about the Sarabanda is its rhythmic similarity to the Chaconne, the first two measures played with the same kind of overdotting, which serves both to propel the piece and to give the second quarter-note its characteristic syncopated emphasis:

5. Here, I should comment that I take issue with those who, evidently intent on improving Bach's work ("gilding the lily"), take the liberty of embellishing certain passages in the Italian style, or advocating the practice. Whereas there is plenty of Baroque repertoire that requires fleshing out in this manner, I consider it to be in poor taste to add notes other than the occasional conventional trill to music as fully realized as are these compositions.

In some editions, the eighth-notes in the third measure are slurred, possibly because of the quarter-notes in the lower voices. This is unnecessary and robs the phrase of its dramatic strength. As explained earlier, Bach's use of quarter-notes here is compositional and may be thought of as suggestive merely of the prevailing degree of energy: note, by way of comparison, the use of the accompanying eighth-notes in mm. 18 and 19. Once again, it is important to clarify the melodic line by releasing the accompanying voice: never sustain a secondary note just because you can, but always tailor its length to the affect.

In this regard, the movement is an interesting case study in note length. There is a progression of double-stops that bestows considerable importance on the second voice: the soprano line is always primary, but the second or alto voice creates significant harmonic tension and merits careful attention to the length of each note. Of course, one other way of conferring predominance on the principal melodic voice in any passage is dynamic shading, whereby that voice receives more bow weight than its accompaniment. In these passages, therefore, favor the soprano line:

In the first two bars, the soprano voice should predominate melodically, but the progression from the third (B-flat/G) to the second (A/G) is harmonically interesting, and the double-stops may be sustained until the eighth-note pickups release the tension.

The trill in the measure after the double bar may be started from the note above or the main note. At this time, most trills would be of the first kind, but in this case, one could argue that it is more effective to sustain the augmented fourth (C-sharp/G) before adding the trill. Of course, because there is a repeat, one may choose to play both versions.

Continue to focus on the double-stops, written and implied, throughout the movement. Awareness of harmonic progression is essential to the understanding and shaping of the music, but the double-stops are such an important motivic element here as to warrant particular attention.

One generally hears what is, in my opinion, a misinterpretation of mm. 12 and 13:

Admittedly, the three sixteenth-notes following the suspension appear to continue over the bar line, but it makes no sense in a Sarabande to create what is effectively a $\frac{4}{4}$ measure followed by one in $\frac{5}{4}$. However, if one hears the final sixteenth-note as a chord tone, the resolution of the passing dissonances, the following phrasing results:

The Accompaniment in "Unaccompanied" Bach

In the following example (mm. 19–22), there is a crescendo through the double-stops to the two four-note chords. Then in m. 22, Bach expands the chord in an arpeggio that could be interpreted in either of two ways, *forte* or *piano*.[6] In the repeat, because of the reflective nature of the coda, one might choose to use *forte* the first time and *piano* on the return.

The coda has a subdued character, and for that reason, in order to keep the tone color dark, it is better not to use the E-string:

---

6. *Subito p* is an unusual dynamic indication at this time, being more associated with the music of composers such as Carl Philipp Emanuel Bach than his father, but it seems to me that such an effect may be effective at such a dramatic point.

CHAPTER EIGHT

The Virtuoso Movements

One word of caution: with the possible exception of the finale of the C-major Sonata, with its constant pedal-like sixteenth-note thread, none of these movements is a *moto perpetuo*. If one thinks of "presto" as meaning "as fast as possible," it's preferable and more effective to translate that as "as fast as the music will tolerate." By this, I mean that it is very important to punctuate this movement so as to allow the music to breathe.

G-Minor Sonata: Presto

Inasmuch as the metronome would not be invented for another hundred years, composers had to use other methods of tempo indication. In my opinion, Bach gave a clear signal about tempo in his choice of time signature. His "³⁄₈" indication looks foreign to our eyes when coupled to what is clearly a ⁶⁄₈ metre. And yet, throughout the movement he alternates long and short bar lines, another unusual but significant practice. The organization of the music in this way indicates a kind of *alla breve*, with the second ³⁄₈ measure weaker than the first, as it would be had he used ⁶⁄₈ as his time signature. In ³⁄₈, the basic unit is the eighth-note; in ⁶⁄₈, it is the half measure, which would suggest a faster tempo.

One fairly common error in performance is the "tripletizing" of the sixteenth-notes:

This is obviously incorrect: the metre is 3/8, not 6/16, and besides, it's impossible to maintain the tripletizing throughout the movement, which results in a bizarre metrical mélange. The metrically correct rendition is:

Performing it in this way—being aware of the correct metrical accents and organizing the music as described above—also has the effect of keeping the tempo in check. Half-barring also helps one understand the phrasing: V–I–V–I sequences can be ambiguous:

In m. 15, the slur, which is ambiguous in the manuscript, should for violinistic reasons be extended to cover the downbeat A as well. The harmonic motion has a leisurely character throughout the movement—organizing the music in the following way helps to reinforce that perception:

Articulations play a substantial role in the enlivenment of music: to repeat, always bear in mind that slurs in this music are not to be regarded as bowings but as part of the language and an essential ingredient of the texture and, consequently, should never be altered or omitted for convenience. Beyond this, the manner of their execution is critical, a reflection of the varying degrees of energy. Bach has fairly sprinkled this particular movement with slurs, and where there are none, there is energetic arpeggiation. The virtuosity, then, has less to do with velocity as with the enjoyment and artistic exploitation of the articulations.

B-Minor Corrente—Double

The *Presto* tempo marking for this movement is deceptive. Note that Bach no longer uses the half-barring system of the Corrente: this indicates that despite the fast triple pulse of the Double, the quarter-notes of the Corrente's duple metre actually move at the same speed or even slightly faster. So, there can be little tempo change between the Corrente and its Double, but the effect is a kaleidoscopic blur of notes, a swift improvisation on the harmonic structure. As I remarked in the commentary on the G-minor Presto, one might think of "presto" as meaning "as fast as possible," which doesn't necessarily mean *technically* but, ideally, "as fast as the *music* will permit." Rather than focusing on the rapidity of the individual notes, then, enjoy the leisurely flow of the harmonies, with a sense of coasting from one impulse to the next:

Because of the rapid tempo, there are some awkward moments. Here are some fingering suggestions:

The A-Minor Finale

The finale of the A-minor Sonata recalls the energy of the Fuga. Its upward-leaping gestures and fleet figuration propel the piece and create an affect of excitement and joie de vivre, enhanced by its quicksilver switches of dynamic. Arpeggiated figures such as those in the opening bar punctuate the movement, and the motivic sixteenth-thirty-second-note figure introduced in m. 2 leaps around the violin like a young gazelle in a number of patterns, some slurred, some detached. Bach has varied the articulation of this figure, but the addition throughout of slurs in m. 3, and so forth, as found in some editions, only detracts from the excitement:

For lightness of execution of this figure, it is essential not to stress each sixteenth-note:

In the interest of clarity, stay in the lowest possible position, using string crossings despite their counterintuitive awkwardness, and remembering also that each slur means a diminuendo. The result is far more exciting:

Here are some more fingering suggestions:

In the following excerpt, I have used staccato dots, wedges, and stress marks to demonstrate the kind of articulation suggested by Bach's liberal use of slurs. Note that one should avoid using the hook-stroke, which tends to flatten the music out and stifle resonance, but always bow as it comes:

Don't lose courage in the coda, with its *piano* dynamic, and feel it necessary to return to *forte* to end the piece. If Bach had intended this, he would hardly have placed the last note abruptly two octaves below the previous one. Instead, approach the coda as though the movement were going to finish with a strong cadence; hesitate slightly before the *subito piano*; then, as the chromatic line descends, let the music gradually ebb away, with a gentle swell in the penultimate measure, a tiny *ritardando*, and a placement of the final A. Above all, *do not vibrate on the A*, but instead, use your bow to shape the note in such a way as to end the piece with delicate expression and a peaceful affect.

The C-Major *Allegro assai*

I always liken the *Allegro assai* of the C-major Sonata to dessert: having worked so hard in the previous three movements, one can unwind and revel in the finale's joyous affect. There is a sensation of buoyancy, of floating or gliding from harmony to harmony that derives from Bach's pervasive use of pedal tones. The piece should be tossed off as lightly and effortlessly as possible.

In the opening gesture, the separate eighth-note is a rebound from the slurred group to the first note of the gesture, not a pickup to the following sixteenth-notes.

This will happen automatically if one is aware of the movement's motivic *alla breve* organization: with only one harmony per measure, there is no secondary beat until the next bar. The first four bars function as an introduction to the initial pedal-tone passage, which can be played a little softer than its repetition, which leads to a two-measure decrescendo. Throughout the movement the dynamic structure tends to parallel the tessitura. Always be on the lookout for the kind of subtle variation that happens in m. 19, and also in mm. 69–72—the G should stand out; once again, mm. 18 and 19 are more effective if played a little louder than the previous pair:

It is generally better to avoid changing position under a slur, and in this case, the fingering I have suggested is in accordance with the phrasing organization, encouraging a slight placement of the downbeat G:

The passage that begins in m. 47 has some awkward moments for fingering. Here are some suggestions:

And later,

The passage starting in m. 69 involves reversed bowing in several bars. Taking it always as it comes, ignoring occasional awkwardness of string crossing, one arrives at m. 84 the right way around. Don't add slurs for the sake of comfort: we should never forget that Bach was an accomplished violinist, but assume that he knew what he was doing and trust his judgment.

I have heard the following passage played with a diminuendo as it rises to sixth position, with the highest notes played *piano*. In terms of Baroque musical language, this is quite inappropriate, for mm. 88–92 constitute, after all, the climax of the movement. In general, an ascending line suggests a crescendo and a descending one a diminuendo. There will be exceptions, of course, but here, the context points strongly toward a climactic rendition:

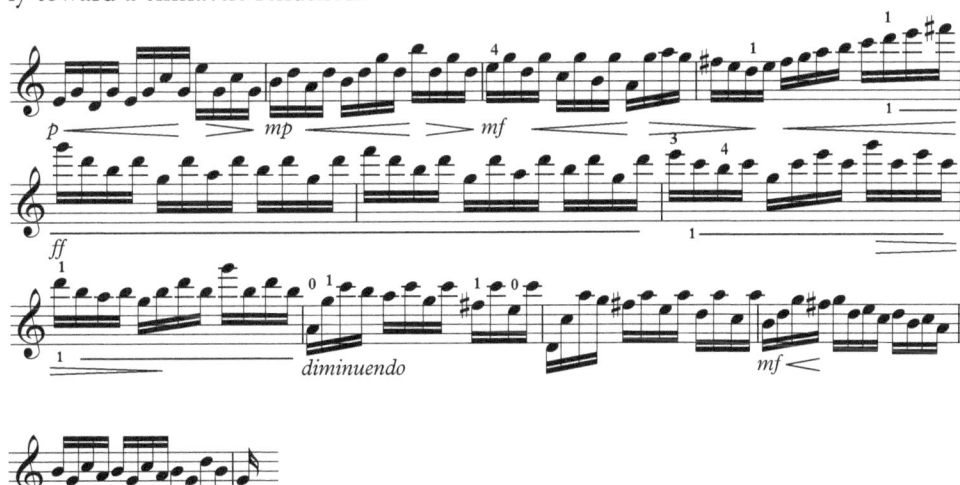

Finish the piece, punctuated as I've suggested for the end of the first section, strongly and without a hint of *ritardando*.

The E-Major Preludio

The organ version of this movement has an orchestral accompaniment: there is a percussive downbeat that launches the solo. In the violin version, it helps to imagine this chord. The most natural way to begin, then, is up-bow:

This is a turbulent piece, with a lot of opportunity for dramatic dynamic shaping:

In choosing a fingering for this passage, it is important to observe the way in which Bach introduces the open E-string, and the actual placement of the *forte*, where the new gesture begins:

The following gesture in *piano* starts on the second eighth-note of the measure.

In the chapter 11, "Right-Hand Technique," I suggest a way to practice the *bariolage* passage that follows. It is important to play it with a smooth arm motion: there's no point in practicing it in an angular way, thinking of each string. The passage begins with a three-measure crescendo, with a slight diminuendo in the fourth; then, in the descending sequential 7–6 progression *forte*, lean on each seventh and relax on the sixths:

In the passage immediately following, take advantage of the figuration to enliven the upward motion:

While playing this passage, and each similar one, focus on these notes within the suggested dynamic pattern:

I do not subscribe to a traditional conception of dynamics in m. 39 and the similar place in m. 102, whereby the downbeat is played softly and the second *sforzando* as the beginning of a gesture. Certainly, the octave leap is dramatic and causes the basic structure of the bar to be short-long and, therefore, the second quarter-note may be dynamically equal to the first, but I think it's an error to treat the downbeat as a resolution.

Note that m. 54 is *not* an echo—the change of pattern calls for a stronger dynamic, the second element of a crescendo to m. 55:

In mm. 94–97, accent the first note of each group to bring out the melodic gestures:

As with the similar section in the *Ciaccona*, the passage from m. 109 to m. 132 makes use of *ondeggiando* bowing: blur the string-crossing with overlegato so as to make the transition as smooth as possible, always favoring the moving voice dynamically and underplaying the pedal. There will, effectively, be a brief double-stop each time.

In the descending sequence, mm. 123–127, focus once again on these notes to produce the liveliest effect:

Be careful to observe the correct inflection of the hemiola—the cadential device Bach uses in mm. 134–135 wherein two bars of ¾ become one in 3/2. The last three measures may be played slightly more spaciously than tempo primo, but imagine the final bar as a graceful harpsichord arpeggio, and play it *senza ritardando* with a slight lengthening of the first note and possibly a diminuendo.

Remember that this is a prelude and, consequently, that it is normal to "segue" into the next movement. Unless there's a very good reason to stop, then, such as needing to tune the instrument, it is most effective to treat the silence following the arpeggio as the first bar of the Loure.

CHAPTER NINE

The Philosophical Movements

The Allemanda

The Allemande was likened by Walther in 1732 to a rhetorical *"Proposition, woraus die übrigen Suiten, als die Courante, Sarabande, und Gigue, als Partes fliessen."*[1] Thirty years later, Marpurg referred to the Allemande as similar to the Prelude.[2] This is precisely the way in which I view the two Allemandas, inasmuch as the character of these movements is not so dance-like in the rhythmic sense, but more of the nature of an introduction—a philosophical piece that precedes the actual dances.

B-Minor Allemanda

For all its stateliness and nobility of spirit, the appearance of this Allemanda, with its dotted rhythms, belies its essential lyricism. I often hear it referred to as a French Overture, which it certainly isn't, or that it should be played in the style of one, rather staccato and energized, with which I respectfully disagree. The confusion most probably stems from a misunderstanding about the variable nature of dotted rhythms in Baroque music. The dotted eighth-sixteenth figure is susceptible to a variety of interpretations according to context. Certainly in a vigorous context, as in many French overtures, the rendition will be crisp and the dot lengthened even to the extent of "double-dotting."[3] At the other extreme, as in the B-minor Corrente, the figure may be played as a triplet.[4]

Before examining the dotted passages, though, let's look at the chords in the opening measures, each of which needs to be rolled quite concisely from the bass note,

---

1. J. G. Walther, *Musicalisches Lexicon, oder Musicalische Bibliothec* (Leipzig, 1732).
2. F. W. Marpurg, *Clavierstücke mit einem practischen Unterricht, i–iii* (Berlin, 1762–1763).
3. This idea was proposed by Leopold Mozart (op. cit.) as an explanation of the normal way of rendering dotted rhythms in his time. It is much more customary now to refer to the practice as "overdotting," thereby avoiding a sense of mathematical strictness.
4. Our familiar long-short triplet figure in a duple metre was virtually never used until well into the nineteenth century, and the dotted eighth-sixteenth notation can frequently be read in this way.

which is on the beat.[5] Once more, the choice of appropriate length of the voices is critical: prolong the upper voice slightly, but note that there is also melodic interest in the alto, so be careful not to pass too rapidly to the E-string, but linger long enough on the A-string for this to be perceptible.

The thirty-second-notes after the trill may be interpreted correctly as a *Nachschlag*, slurred into the trill, or else bowed separately—an artistic decision. On the other hand, it should be noted that similar pairs of thirty-seconds occur throughout the movement and could thereby acquire the status of a motivic figure. Slurring them each time would deprive the movement of a lot of its energy, and my preference is always to play them separately. The fact that Bach does occasionally slur them need not necessarily, I feel, be interpreted as an indication that he intended others to be treated similarly. Here's my bowing solution for the opening measures:

When using Z-bowing on extended passages, the bow direction often needs to be adjusted: the idea is to flow from one end to the other with continual arm motion, acknowledging the contours of the phrase:

The lines symbolize constant bow direction: the arm never stops moving.

Here's an experiment that explains my perception of the function of the dotted rhythms in this movement: Play the opening phrase, substituting equal legato eighth-notes for the dotted figures: the effect is quite different, rather stately and measured, the music seeming to move more slowly, and yet not implausibly so. Then restore the dots, being careful not to stiffen the rhythm staccato-style, but still playing the notes legato and as they come.[6] As I see it, the effect of the dotted rhythm is to make the music flow easily, and in order to facilitate this, I make use of "Z-bowing" (a technique described in chapter 11, "Right-Hand Technique") to create a flowing legato line but with varying energy according to context. Whereas triplet rendition of the dotted figures in this movement would sound lazy, excessive overdotting will make it jerky; when it is played using Z-bowing, and being careful to play the sixteenth-note lightly, one can achieve an effective interpretation without consciously altering the written rhythm.

---

5. See the discussion of chordal technique in chapter 11.

6. In my opinion, the "hook-stroke" is not to be used in the music of Bach, nor in that of any other Baroque composer for that matter.

The Allemande's "philosophical" nature to which I allude is best communicated in a spontaneous, conversational performing style, something Bach facilitates already by organizing the music in units of irregular length:

To achieve spontaneity while still maintaining the stately affect, use subtle *rubato* to avoid rigid adherence to written note values. In the following passage, for example, try slightly extending the first two dotted sixteenth-notes, hesitating for a moment on the top A, then allowing the music to move forward to the middle of the next bar, poising there before flowing easily as far as the E-major 6/3 on the downbeat of m. 4, and using the triplets as the beginning of the cadential gesture. I include suggestions of dynamics, bowings, and phrasing of the sort that may be applied throughout the movement to transmit the dramatic changes of character:

In the second half of the movement, there are several places that demonstrate the kind of low-position fingerings necessary to preserve polyphonic tone-color. Notice, also, that the chord on the third quarter of m. 16 must be arpeggiated upward to the C so that the soprano phrase-unit is completed. It is not necessary to break the chord downward in order to sustain the A: after all, each voice in the chord is a dotted eighth-note, and the mandatory beaming is merely compositional, not an indication of the playing length of the bass note. This happens numerous times in these works, and the solution, as I have suggested elsewhere, is to lean more on the bass note and then make a vertical diminuendo, prolonging the soprano note.

This movement, along with the G-minor Adagio and the A-minor Grave, is notable for the complexity of its figuration. It is particularly important in this type of writing to reduce the voices, at least mentally, to basic unornamented lines in order to understand which notes are principally melodic. Here is a sample of the kind of melodic reduction done by students in my course. Suggestions for punctuation are indicated with commas; as in the first section, dynamics and nuances should be based on the melodic and harmonic structure.

One of the most important tenets of Baroque performance style is that of stress versus release, or "good" notes versus "bad." We speak of "tossing notes away," which is achieved by subtle adjustments of the weight of the bow and the speed of the stroke as well as the judicious use of agogic accents (the lengthening of notes) and *rubato*. Focusing on basic melodic notes such as these encourages one to play subsidiary notes with appropriate lightness. Bow division, graduated and varied according to the dynamic context, is an essential component of intelligent interpretation: beware of falling into the trap of automatically using as much bow as possible. Basic stylistic elements that characterize a "Romantic" approach to interpretation, as opposed to an "Early Music" one, are the greater use of *legato* or *sostenuto* bow strokes and the tendency to give too much importance to notes that would normally have been tossed away lightly. Of course, technique and style evolves from one musical period to the next, and the Tourte-style bow encourages that manner of playing. The application of the performance practice of one period or geographic location to the music of another, however, usually results in a confused and confusing mismatch.

What matters most in this aspect of Baroque performance practice is that each "sound" (i.e., a single note or two or more slurred notes) be shaped and separated from its neighbors. In both fast and lyrical passages, the bow or string change itself will often suffice, but subtle, artistic right-hand technique calls for constant awareness of the necessary gradations of pressure and release—pressure applied by the index finger and release controlled by the little finger—and of varied stroke speed and length, of particular point of contact, of arm weight, and the part of the bow best suited to the requisite degree of articulation.

D-Minor Allemanda

The monophonic style of composition of the opening bar disguises an important element of its basic harmonic structure that is usually overlooked. If one hears the correct chordal progression, though, the following becomes apparent:

Notice that the first harmony, D-minor, lasts until the B-flat, which is an anticipation of the diminished-seventh: because of this, I recommend the following fingering:

Whereas the suggested fingering may seem somewhat awkward because of the string-crossing, the real harmony emerges more readily, and the resultant tonal clarity is preferable, for despite the monophonic writing, this is still polyphonic music.

With regard to the harmonic progression, I would also draw your attention to mm. 15 and 23, where analogous motivic figures occur, the difference being that in these the final note of the second quarter leaps down a major sixth instead of rising.

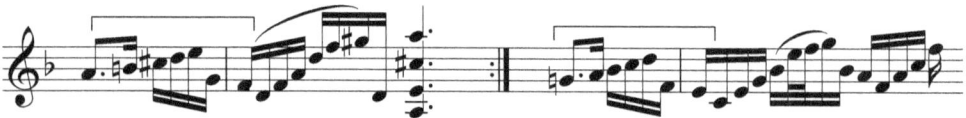

Threaded through the sixteenth-notes, then, are vocal lines that should be clearly perceived by the player if the phrasing is to be understood. As ever, the bass line is the most important, because it supports the harmonies and defines their duration. The bass notes will not always occur at the beginning of a harmony, and must even be inferred at times. Here is an example of a possible bass-line extraction:

The short slurred figures—two, three, and four notes—are textural features throughout the movement. In a few places, however, Bach wrote longer slurs that are to be respected: one frequently hears performances in which the ones in mm. 9 and 10 are broken for convenience. However, this destroys their special function: sixteen notes slurred will sound noticeably softer than eight, and the four-note slur that begins the descending sequence will be still louder. Consequently, by using articulations of decreasing length, Bach has written a crescendo whose effect is destroyed when the slurs are broken.[7] It is advisable to stay as low in the bow as comfortable while the sequence winds down so as to prepare for the three separate sixteenths that precede the long slur. Note as well that the first three notes of the long slur are also the last three notes of the preceding sequence:

---

7. How strange that a modern violinist would find it too uncomfortable to play sixteen notes in one Tourte-style bow, which is noticeably longer than the type of bow with which Bach was familiar.

The rule about a slur meaning a diminuendo must be qualified here: obviously, a group of eight or sixteen notes slurred will need to be shaped appropriately. I prefer to say that a slur will mean a diminuendo *sooner or later*. In other words, there will be an immediate diminuendo in a short slur, but in longer ones, it will occur later depending on the shape of the gesture, even if it happens on the very last note.

Here again, in the descending sequences in mm. 11–12 and 20–21, avoid the use of the hook-stroke, which has a stifling effect on the sound; in such passages, always take the bowing as it comes. In our quasi-Romantic approach, an effort is made to suppress the natural accent suggested by Bach's choice of articulation, but there is nothing at all wrong with the syncopated effect that this produces: Bach seems to have liked off-beat accentuation, an excellent example being the opening bars of the prelude to his sixth cello suite. In any case, the ability to play a fast *piano* bow stroke in either direction, but especially up-bow, is essential.

The energetic figures in mm. 14 and 21 should be played in such a way as to avoid equal accentuation—keep the up-bows, which return to the melodic note, lighter than the down-bows.[8] The interpolated gesture after the double bar should be clearly separated from the new phrase that follows. Here are some suggestions of fingering and dynamics:

---

8. The way I explain this type of gesture to my students is that the combined down-up bow strokes are to be considered as one: the stroke—a continuous arm motion—starts and ends in the same place. To execute this effectively the arm must be slightly more elevated on the return and not on the same plane: the motion is effectively elliptical.

CHAPTER TEN

The Lyrical Movements

The Siciliana

This term was commonly used to refer to an aria type and instrumental movement popular in the late seventeenth and eighteenth centuries, and often to a dance commonly considered a form of slow Gigue. In the eighteenth century, the *Siciliana* was associated with pastoral scenes and melancholy emotions. It was as a dance, however, that the Siciliana was known to eighteenth-century theorists, Mattheson suggesting that it be performed slowly and used to evoke melancholy passions. As the metre of this movement is $\frac{12}{8}$, it should not be played too slowly but in an easily flowing tempo. To enhance the impression of flow, there is a customary alteration of the written rhythm, whereby the dotted eighth-note is subtly prolonged and the sixteenth delayed:

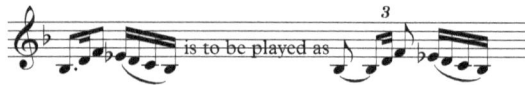

The movement is written as a conversational trio for one lower voice and two upper. The upper voices answer at first, but in the middle of m. 4, the opening gesture might be heard as a cadential figure, after which the roles are reversed:

Whereas the separate eighth-notes in the upper voices are relatively lyrical, the accompanying bass eighth-notes should be lightly articulated, similar to pizzicato in effect, so as to promote an easy flow and to provide impulses out of which spring the melodic voices. The bow should release the string in such a way as to give each one a resonant quality.

Once again, in m. 9, Bach uses the opening figure as a cadence, this time in the relative minor. Note that the separate up-bow on the thirty-second-note B-flat in m. 8 identifies it as part of the bass line and should therefore be rendered in the same way as the eighth-notes:

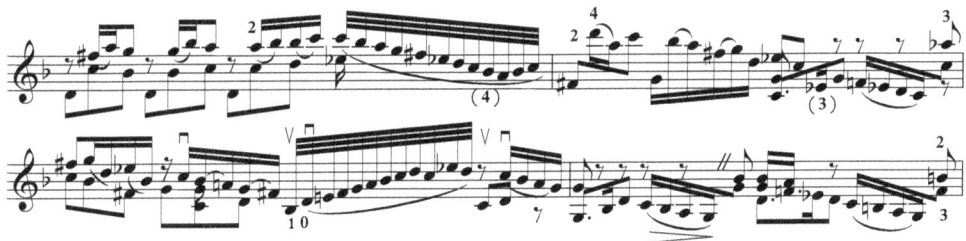

The fingerings suggested are designed to maintain a clear differentiation of tone color in order to keep the voices as independent as possible.[1] For most of the movement, the four descending slurred sixteenth-note figure falls away dynamically. The only place where they are not slurred is in m. 15, during the climactic passage, where a crescendo seems more appropriate:

To avoid stiffness and angularity, *Siciliana*-style rhythmic alteration can also be used in these and similar figures:

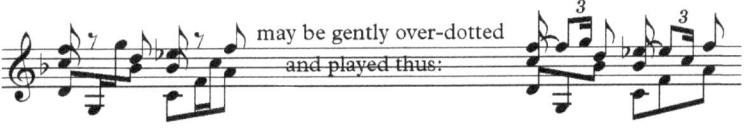

---

1. This is an important aesthetic consideration in the interpretation of polyphony. Wherever possible, one should avoid noticeable changes of vocal tone-color in midphrase, which explains certain position changes that may seem unnecessary.

A-Minor Sonata: Andante

It seems to me that Bach has, perhaps, borrowed from Vivaldi for this piece, which resembles stylistically a typical slow movement in one of that composer's concertos, where a constant eighth-note pulse accompanies a cantabile melodic line. The melody itself is simple and singable, and it is important to remember that in eighteenth-century music, the word *andante* does not infer slow tempo but, rather, at a pace that's easily flowing without hurrying. Generally, Andantes move steadily forward with only occasional, minimal use of *rubato*. Chords must always be broken after the beat or arpeggiated from it, for the bass note *is* the beat and its constant motion of the bass line is the primary motivic element of this movement. The accompanying eighth-notes should be evenly articulated throughout—a brushed détaché—never with a variety of lengths. There is no need, however, for melodic eighth-notes to be short to match the accompaniment: these need to be played lyrically. This movement, with its bivocal scoring, realizes so clearly the aesthetic goal of making one player sound like more than one.

The sustained melodic notes require two or three of the accompanying eighth-notes to be played in the same direction. For example,

In the first bar, release the quarter-note only as you begin the following eighth—the bow change is all the articulation needed. Above all, don't protract or sustain any of the eighth-notes. Some modern editions have editorial slurs added, but in my opinion, it's better to leave Bach's version intact the first time through—he did, after all, use slurs in nine places—and then add some spontaneous articulations on the repeat. Besides, one can shape the unslurred gestures quite beautifully with a subtle *détaché*, and the added articulations in the repeat then will be much more effective.

Here's a sample of the kind of ornamental slurring that might be appropriate, connecting notes that have something in common: grouping, direction, or harmony. Above all, vary the duration of the added slurs, not just two-and-two throughout, and concentrate on maintaining the quasi-hypnotic quality of the repeated eighths:

In the final measures of the movement, the third quarter-note of m. 24 is in the nature of a question, so a slight placement of the final F-sharp is in order, especially at the end of the movement, and the cadential gesture needs to be slurred:

The C-Major Sonata: Largo

I always think of Largo as denoting Cantabile, and the main difference between the Largo and the Andante, besides being a trifle slower, is that this movement is more flexible, spacious, and *arioso*. In this piece, the repeated eighths are certainly lyrical, and the absence of constant pulsation means that there can be a more conversational flavor to the phrase structure. There are also numerous *Luftpausen*, phrasing punctuations, and rhetorical silences, and the affect is tender. In mm. 6 and 16, a rhetorical silence precedes the ascending sequence that leads to the final cadence of each section. Take time to place the first note of this phrase to enhance its poignancy, and for that reason, separate each sequential element slightly from the next, especially in the coda.

Here is one idea of the kind of expression suggested by the gestures and sequential elements:

Eighth-notes accompanying slurred sixteenths often need to be played shorter than the sixteenths so as not to confuse the vocal separation. Typical instances are those in mm. 2, 6, and 7: failure to release the eighths in time causes an elision of the two voices.

Despite the lyricism of this movement, the articulations need to be clear and the "sounds" more spoken than sung. By this I mean that special attention should be paid to the tapering of slurs and to the gentle separation, for example, of pairs of slurred sixteenths from each other. The amount of separation will depend on whether the pairs are moving in a smooth direction or in a broken line. In the opening passage, for example, the broken intervals in m. 1 need to be more articulated than the ascending pairs in m. 2 or the arching ones in m. 3.

Separate sixteenth-notes, such as those in mm. 4 and 5, should have a consonant's spoken clarity but not be played equally, the "on-beat" ones being slightly stronger than the "off-beat." This example demonstrates the way in which such inflections occur during larger dynamic shapes, as well as the appropriate playing lengths of accompanying eighth-notes:

At the time this music was composed, trills generally started from the upper note and were essentially a series of appoggiaturas. Because the trill in the above example starts on B-flat, the preceding note, also B-flat, should be played more softly so as not to upstage the appoggiatura. The trills in mm. 2 and 8 occur on notes that are already dissonant, so that the upper notes create an octave and a fifth, respectively, with the bass.[2] In my opinion, the trills should therefore be played after the main note and be quite brief—a couple of notes will suffice.

When two notes that descend one step are slurred and the second one is trilled, the tied note becomes the upper note of the trill. This example illustrates the way that each of these trills are realized:

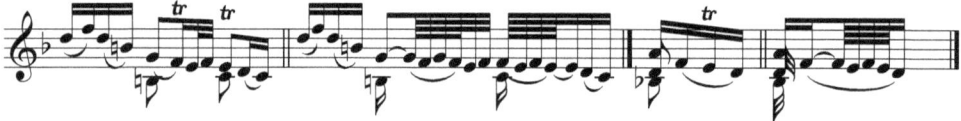

In the last four measures, having denied the listener the expected final cadential chord, Bach inserts a gently reflective melismatic phrase. At this point, when we're once again expecting the final cadence, two readings are possible: one shocks us with a dramatic diminished-seventh chord, ending this otherwise-peaceful move-

2. The perfect fourth is considered to be a dissonance.

ment with a strong gesture that propels the work into its exuberant finale; the other possible ending is, maintaining the prevailing affect. Here are both:

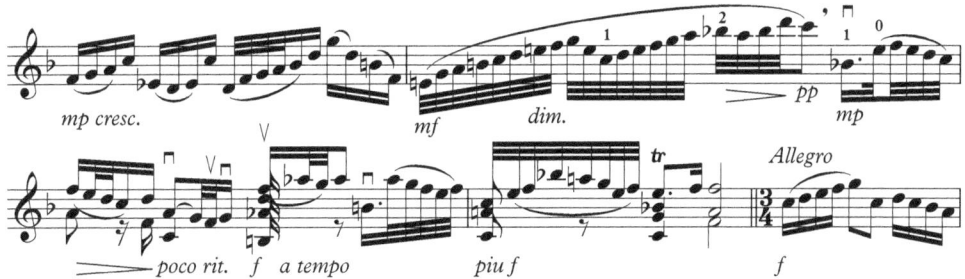

Or else, perhaps

There is absolutely no need to break the slur over the longer melisma, which is simply an improvisatory ornamental flourish: just let it flow forward easily after a brief sustaining of the E, accelerate slightly, then fall back at the end.

CHAPTER ELEVEN

Right-Hand Technique

The final two chapters of this book are substantially identical to material in my previous volume, *Before the Chinrest—A Guide to the Mysteries of Pre-Chinrest Technique and Style* (Indiana University Press, 2012), but treat much of what has been discussed herein in greater depth. The first book was directed at those wishing to experiment with and become proficient in the use of the earlier instrument and bow, but "modern" violinists often discover that certain "Baroque" concepts are transferable and actually facilitate technical execution on their own instruments. With this in mind, then, these two chapters summarize ideas that have been discussed or alluded to throughout, or expand them, and I apologize for any perceived redundancy.

The Sonatas and Partitas pose challenges that require a special right-hand technique, and I shall devote this chapter to a discussion of specific issues encountered in polyphonic and dance music. First, though, a word about the subtleties of Baroque style: when playing the music of the seventeenth and eighteenth centuries, whether using a modern or a pre-Tourte bow, one must understand that there is a need for the shaping of individual sounds that exceeds the usual demands of nineteenth- and twentieth-century repertoire. It seems that students today are exhorted to use as much bow as possible, without much regard for subtleties of right-hand expression that are desirable in pre-Romantic music. The elements of what I refer to as the "choreography" of bow strokes—the careful variation of point of contact, the intelligent planning of bow division, the artistic choice of note length, the subtle application of tone colors—all contribute to what is effectively a "spoken" approach to interpretation, as well as to the more usual and traditional "sung." Awareness of the importance of the alternation of vowels and consonants in the texture, which calls for delicate right-hand control, is another essential ingredient in any successful interpretation in Baroque and Classical style.

There is evidently a school of technique that promotes a bow grip with fingers spread apart, claw-like, in such a way that flexible use of the joints is impossible. In my teaching, I stress the need for a loose support of the bow, thumb relaxed, and fingers separated no more than they are when the arm is hanging at one's side. In that way, the index and fourth fingers can be ready for those moments when inflection or adjustments of balance are called for. In the music of Bach and his contemporaries and antecedents, it is not only necessary to pay particular attention to the variety of bow speed and division but also to the function of the index finger in applying pressure and the little finger in controlling the weight of the bow.

Variety of articulation is a critical factor. Just think of it this way: each individual note constitutes a single sound, as do a group of slurred notes—the more notes under a slur, the less energetic that particular sound. I generally apply Leopold Mozart's dictum: the first note under a slur is the loudest and each successive note softer.[1] Obviously, there are qualifications to this rule, which mainly applies to groups of two or more notes moving in the same direction. Personally, I prefer to say that a slur implies a diminuendo *sooner or later*. That means that notes under a slur may be shaped according to context, but that the last note—the end of that sound—will always be separated from the next sound to a greater or lesser degree.

This is an important tenet of Baroque and Classical performance practice and one of the most significant differences between that and "Romantic" style. String players are taught that bow changes should generally be imperceptible, and as students we strive to achieve that aesthetic goal. Granted, the technique is valuable in certain contexts, especially for the sustaining of notes that cannot possibly be played in one bow (a comparative rarity in Baroque music). However, this way of playing is alien to the eighteenth-century concept of articulation, and when applied to Baroque and Classical repertoire only succeeds in making it sound smooth and flattened out, and often—contributing to what is most unfortunate—like weak Romantic music.[2]

Polyphony

It is essential to recognize that Bach is constantly writing polyphonically, even in apparently homophonic passages, and that this is the reason for his assigning individual stems to each note in a double-stop or chord. These are simply vocal coincidences—points at which two, three, or four voices coincide—and the principal melodic line may occur in any voice, which occasions a special right-hand technique. It is most important to avoid accenting chords unduly, perceiving them as special events in the texture, unless the harmonic or rhetorical structure of the music calls for it: treat each voice in such a way as to support the melodic flow, and not disrupt it by needless overemphasis.

Chordal Technique

There are a number of principles to bear in mind when playing chords in Baroque style. Here are my suggestions concerning the technique of chord playing:

1. Always keep your elbow low—let the arm hang loosely.

---

1. Op. cit.
2. In my teaching, I refer to this, the unwarranted smooth transition from one bow stroke to another, as the "peanut butter syndrome."

2. The fingers and wrist should be relaxed: it is essential for the production of a full, resonant, and unforced tone that the bow be supported but not gripped.
3. At the beginning of a movement or after a silence, never start a chord with the bow on the string, but come from the air at an oblique angle.
4. Don't put the bow on the lowest string by raising your elbow, but rather allow the bow to fall there under its own weight by relaxing the pressure of the fourth finger, being sure that the upper arm follows in the direction that the bow, hand, and forearm have taken but does not lead: never raise it to place the bow on the bass note. You'll find that this technique produces a firm yet unforced bass note for the chord.
5. The fingers should always point away from the direction of the stroke: when playing a down-bow chord, let the wrist lead and the fingers trail behind.
6. When playing a chord down-bow, the stroke should be generated by allowing the elbow to fall, with the forearm and hand following.
7. When playing a chord up-bow, make the stroke by letting the elbow fall inward toward your ribs.

Chord playing in Baroque music involves a degree of arpeggiation dictated by context. The way of "breaking" a chord as used in the opening Allegro of the Bruch G minor Concerto is, in my opinion, inappropriate in Baroque music, as are two other methods. In my teaching I have nicknamed each of them.

The first:

I call "ta-WHA!" as in:

The second:

I call "ha-CHOO!" as in:

And the third:

I call "ta-wha-CHOO!" (a combination of the other two) as in the continuation of the previous passage:

None of these is appropriate. One should remember, when performing chords in Baroque music that each one is comprised of two or three individual double-stops. For instance, when a four-note chord is played as a "ta-WHA!" only the outer two double-stops are heard—the middle one is inaudible. In principle, then, the appropriate way to play chords in Baroque and in much Classical music is to roll them upward from the bass note, *which must always be placed on the beat*, the degree of arpeggiation dictated by affect, tempo, dynamic, and function in the overall context. Certainly, there are times when a chord needs to be percussive or crisply played with little noticeable arpeggiation, but the styles of breaking I have described above are never appropriate.

Context will dictate whether to start rolling a chord from a single note or from a double-stop, and the speed of rolling as well. In a particularly soft or tender moment, one can roll a chord slowly and gently, as a lute player or harpsichordist might. If there is a particularly affecting harmonic shift or unexpected melodic twist, it may be interesting to linger a little on one of the notes. In a declamatory or *vivace* passage, a rapid arpeggiation will usually be appropriate.

When playing polyphonic music, it is possible also to "shade" a chord in such a way as to allow one note to stand out more than the others. If, for instance, one needs to emphasize the bass note, a vertical diminuendo is required; if the tenor is the predominant voice, as in the second phrase of the Ciaccona, start with a double-stop, using the weight of the arm to lean more on the D-string, and then relax the sound on the A and E.

Chords may be played either down-bow or up-bow at any dynamic level. A succession of chords should ideally be played "as they come"—it is better to reserve repeated down-bows for places where the music calls for a percussive, extremely energetic or angry effect.

Finally, the ideal effect in chord playing will be achieved by having the sensation of falling through the strings, not going around the outside of them. In order to do this, keep the hand relaxed and the palm soft, so that the work is being done by arm weight, not finger pressure. Most importantly, never raise the upper arm to make the stroke, but always let the elbow hang.

Here is a simple exercise. Supporting the bow loosely with the thumb, place it on the E-string a little above the frog, then relax and curve your fourth finger to allow the point of the bow to fall until the hair comes to rest on the G-string. Keep your wrist loose, and the weight of the bow will cause the hand to rise and the wrist to straighten. First, do this a few times without allowing the elbow to rise, then, as the bow contacts the G-string, draw a down-bow with the wrist still flat and the relaxed fingers left behind. You will notice that the tone produced in this way is full and resonant.[3]

Next, play a simple legato arpeggio, drawing the bow smoothly across the strings with relaxed hand and wrist, and allowing the arm to fall in a fluid motion:

Then gradually blur the arpeggiation so that the bow touches each string and pair of strings briefly as you lower and raise your arm. Now close your eyes and focus on the sensation of the smooth motion of your arm—rather than planning when you're going to arrive on each string, be surprised when you do:

Don't overlook the fact that you need to play chords up-bow as well as down. This time, feel the smooth motion of the forearm swinging outward, away from the body, during the down-bow, and inward, toward the ribs, for the up-bow:

This technique may be used to good effect in the opening of the *Allemanda* of the B-minor Partita:

---

3. For an excellent exercise in this technique, see Geminiani, op. cit., *Esempio* XVI.

When playing such a passage, try to keep your arm on the plane of the melodic voice, with your hand and wrist relaxed. By releasing the pressure of the fourth finger to allow the bow to fall to the lowest string under its own weight, the bass notes stand out clearly, and the chord is produced with far less effort than when raising the elbow. In this way both the tone quality and the clarity of the polyphony will be enhanced.

Martelé and Spiccato

Neither of these bow strokes is applicable in Baroque performance. Quite apart from being historically inappropriate—in the case of *martelé* the stroke is certainly intended for use with a Tourte-style bow, and it is recorded that *spiccato* was first experimented with in Vienna in the late years of the eighteenth century, regarded as a fad, and soon rejected—neither of these strokes works well with a Baroque bow. Furthermore, even when using a modern bow, a better effect can be achieved by the use of other strokes.

I tell my students that the Baroque bow never stops moving until you put it back in the case. By this I mean simply that the right arm should always be fluid in motion, that one should always make use of the kind of "follow-through" that a golfer or tennis player utilizes in any stroke. Indeed, there is a very good physiological reason for this: just as the follow-through in sport prevents injury that could result from an abrupt cessation of motion, so it is with the string player's right arm, and the use of a stroke that requires a sudden freezing of motion can cause injury. Short sounds can be produced on the violin without the jarring motion of the *martelé*, usually with lifted strokes, but even *staccato* strokes at the point of the bow do not require a sudden stop of the forearm's motion, and can be completed with a "follow-through."

From the musical point of view, any stroke that stifles the resonance of the instrument is really a special effect, one to be used sparingly. For this reason, the hook-stroke, a variation of *martelé*, is generally not appropriate in Baroque music due to its tendency to stifle the resonance of the sound. Unless a special effect of the kind is called for, it is preferable to lift or lighten the bow slightly, and generally bow passages in which you might normally use hook-stroke as it comes. Imagine always that the goal in Baroque-style bow technique is to release the sound from the violin, not forcing or maintaining undue pressure, but causing it to ring like a bell. I tell my students to think of the right hand as a magnet that attracts the sound.

When a passage calls for short notes that sound better played in the upper half of the bow, use the fourth finger to balance it and lighten each stroke, releasing the pressure of the first finger. Once again, be sure to use a fluid, constant arm motion, never stopping the bow between notes. One example is the subject of the G-minor Fuga:

Sautillé

The literal meaning of the word *spiccato* is "distinct." Spiccato, the bow stroke, has no use in Baroque music: the appropriate stroke for sixteenth-note passage work is *sautillé*. To practice sautillé, begin by drawing the bow slowly back and forth on an open string, watching the tip of the bow to make sure that the stroke is continuously horizontal. Then gradually speed up and shorten the stroke, until, in the middle of the bow, rapid, clear notes result with the hair never leaving the string. You'll find that when executing this stroke in the middle of the bow the stick tends to rise and lift the hair from the string, and the harder you press on the bow, the more it fights back. Using this technique, one may vary the degree of articulation according to the mood of a passage by playing further toward the point, where the notes will be less clear; however, the closer to the middle of the bow one plays the clearer and more "spiccato" the effect will be. Most significant, though, allegro sixteenth-notes are to be played *on the string*, not off, because of the natural articulation achieved by the use of sautillé. This instruction is also in accordance with that of Bismantova, in a late-seventeenth treatise, who says that *passaggi* (passages in rapid notes) should be played "with short strokes at the point of the bow."[4]

Bariolage

This is a term that refers to a rapid détaché, usually notated in sixteenth-notes in which the bow passes back and forth between two strings, generally with a repeated open string. One frequently encounters such passages in the music of Vivaldi and Bach. Here is a familiar example in the E-major Preludio:

Obviously, it is important in such a passage to bring out the moving voice and underplay the pedal tone, and the following is an exercise that I prescribe.

Each eighth-note should be played strongly, with pressure by the index finger, and the sixteenths released and played lightly, the pairs of notes grouped as triplets, long-short, long-short. Focus also on pulling the down-bow in a lateral direction, not circular, pivoting around the elbow, which should remain low, the upper arm relaxed.

---

4. Bartolomeo Bismantova, *Compendio musicale* (1677): "*e nel far alle volte passaggi si suona al punta d'arco con l'arcada corta*" (and always, in rapid passages, play at the point of the bow with short strokes).

(As I have remarked elsewhere, each pair of notes constitutes one bow stroke.) Having practiced the exercise slowly for a while, without changing anything else play the passage at the desired tempo, and you'll find that whereas it will no longer be possible to play it in triplets, the melodic voice will now stand out easily from the texture.

This practice method can be applied to all similar passages. Occasionally one will encounter one such as this, in the finale of the C-major Sonata, in which the bowing is reversed. Once again, practice the *bariolage* in triplets, remembering to keep the elbow low and the upper arm relaxed and neutral:

Occasionally, this type of bowing occurs over three strings. This famous passage in the E-major *Preludio* requires a complex, continuous arm motion:

It is most important *not* to think of each string as one plays this passage but rather to concentrate on the two arm motions involved: a lateral movement of the forearm to produce the sound and a vertical one to change the plane of the bow. One very important piece of advice: *Don't try to play each string individually*. In order to arrive at a comfortable, consistent execution, focus solely on achieving a smooth, involuntary, arpeggiated bow stroke, and to do this, it is best to practice at first on open strings. Here's a preparatory exercise:

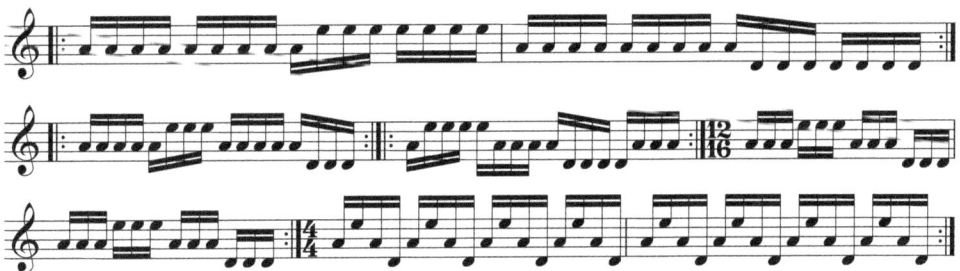

Practice it this way: With the elbow hanging loosely, use an upward and downward motion of the forearm, pivoting around the elbow, to catch the E and D. Repeat the first two measures until the action is involuntary, then go to the subsequent measures and work on each in the same way. The basic purpose of this exercise is to accustom yourself to using your forearm instead of your upper arm for the string-crossings. The elbow will rise and fall, but whereas it is essential that the upper arm be free to move, it should not initiate the action.

There is another exercise that cannot be notated, for it requires random motion: Start by playing rapid repeated sixteenth-notes on the open A string; then, without interrupting the repetition, randomly raise and lower your forearm, gradually reducing the number of notes on each string. Continue in this way, working to achieve the smooth vertical arm motion that results in your being able to play each string only once. At first this will sound chaotic, but the object is to arrive at a fluid execution of the pattern of string-crossing required. These two motions combined are the secret of the smooth execution of this passage.

Ondeggiando

This word means, literally, "swaying," and refers to a legato stroke between two strings that can encompass as few as two notes or as many as sixteen. It requires the use of a free, relaxed wrist so as to allow the hand to make a gentle, vertical waving motion while the forearm moves smoothly back and forth. What is important in general, and especially when there is a pedal tone, is that the pedal tone be unaccented and that the change from one string to the other be slightly blurred, with a brief, virtually inaudible double-stop. It could be notated as follows:

For an exercise, begin by playing a plain open-string fifth a few times and then, with the elbow low, change to a vertical waving motion (*it is important to execute the stroke, wrist relaxed and flexible, by raising the hand, not lowering it*):

It occurs in the G-minor Adagio and also in the Ciaccona:

CHAPTER TWELVE

Left-Hand Technique

Just as there is a type of right-hand technique that facilitates the execution of otherwise-awkward passages in Bach's solo polyphony, there are certain concepts of fingering that I recommend in order to facilitate vocal clarity, tonal homogeneity, and melodic fluency. The difference between fingering that's appropriate in Bach's polyphonic works and in standard, post-Baroque music is the result of changing aesthetic notions. Leopold Mozart did indeed recommend staying on the same string, where possible, to maintain the tonal color in a melodic line. However, whereas this effect is certainly desirable in the case of Bach's fugue subjects, using positions higher than first can actually disrupt a Bachian melodic line or make notes sound abruptly duller. The simplest advice I can give is to stay in the lowest possible position until it's absolutely necessary for musical or technical reasons to use a higher one. Running up a string merely to show off one's technical prowess is shallow and pointless, especially considering the level of virtuosity already required to be able to perform these works. Here's a ludicrous example from a mid-twentieth-century edition of the G-minor Adagio:

Quite apart from the empty virtuosity, from the vocal point of view playing the E-flat on the D-string and then switching over to the A-string for the next note in the melodic line, a fourth lower, thereby introducing a brighter color in mid-phrase, disrupts its homogeneity. Abrupt changes of color in melodic lines, then, are to be avoided; gradual changes such as happen in scales or arpeggios or during sequences are normal. Open strings may be used wherever context permits: in scales, however, the modern practice of using open strings ascending and fourth finger descending is undesirable in this music. Notice, if you will, how this causes the ascending E, especially, to stand out from the texture: the sudden change of color draws attention to that note. An open E used in a descending scale, however, blends into the overall color and the string-crossing is smooth and unnoticeable.

The Role of Vibrato

In approaching music of any period, it is important for the violinist to ponder on the function of vibrato as an expressive tool and not merely an element of tone production. The automatic use of constant unvaried vibrato, applied without concern about its appropriateness or effect, is lamentable and is, in any case, a relatively recent phenomenon in the history of music. Vibrato's origins are lost in the history of style, but from the early Middle Ages when it was first written about until the second decade of the twentieth century, vibrato was understood to be an ornamental device used to enhance the expression of particular notes in the overall context of the music.[1]

It is essential, therefore, for the violinist to develop the ability to use vibrato of varying speed and width in order to have as complete an expressive palette as possible. This seems to have been standard element of violin pedagogy in the eighteenth century: Leopold Mozart[2] and Tartini[3] provided systematic exercises; Geminiani[4] furnished a sampling of styles of vibrato to be applied according to the particular affect desired. However, in the absence of more precise information as must have been conveyed by demonstration—a lost tradition—we are obliged to use our creative instincts.

The guidelines, then, are similar to those for trills. The speed and amplitude of the oscillations should match the character of the affect: fast trills and vibrato should never be used in slow movements.[5] The duration should not only be determined by note length, because the addition of vibrato to a long note, especially when the note is swelled, can be most effective. Avoid using vibrato on expressively weak notes, such as the resolution of a dissonance. Remember also that non-vibrato is as much an expressive device in Baroque music as it is in modern music: for instance, it can evoke affects such as sadness or represent sleep.

Excessively wide vibrato or a nervous flutter can draw attention to itself and detract from the affect of the music. As well as carefully controlled wrist or arm vibrato, I recommend one type of vibrato that serves only to warm the sound: I call it "vertical." It is produced by pressing the finger firmly on the fingerboard and then releasing the pressure without allowing the string to rise. Practice a series of such pulsations, gradually increasing its speed until the motion becomes involuntary, and an almost-imperceptible shimmer of sound results. In this type of vibrato, there should be no rolling of the fingertip—correctly done, it will produce no noticeable alteration of pitch, and the notes to which it is applied will sound warm.

Never forget that the bow is the string player's primary expressive tool and that vibrato plays a secondary role in the interpretative process. In other words, first shape notes and phrases with the bow and then decide which notes in the phrase need to be

---

1. See G. Moens-Haenen's article on vibrato in *Grove Music Online*.
2. Op. cit.
3. *Traité des agrémens de la musique* (Paris, 1770).
4. Op. cit.
5. The automatic "electric bell" style of trill has no place in this music: I tell my students that in the case of trills of short duration, one should always know precisely how many notes to play and practice them slowly and rhythmically, lifting the finger high.

ornamented with vibrato. The artistic application of vibrato in Bach's music will enhance and amplify an affect, but one must first plan the dynamic structure, nuances, and color of each phrase and the bow strokes that shape it.

Half-Position

When playing the music of Bach, one frequently encounters passages that require the use of half-position. Here are some exercises to help you become more comfortable with its use. Be sure to sustain the fingers on the string for as long as indicated:

Choice of Fingerings

There are times when I recommend certain fingerings that may seem unorthodox or counterintuitive. Here is an example of a simple gesture that can be clumsy if fingered without changing position:

In this example, staying in first position requires that the third finger jump sideways, whereas when using the following fingering, there is a sensation of walking instead of jumping, and the continuity of the melodic line is uninterrupted. When trying this, focus on the placement of the second finger, not the third, for the C will be on the beat:

To execute such a maneuver, instead of moving the whole hand, keep your thumb in place and swing your arm to bring your hand to second position, which is also much more comfortable for the ensuing gesture.

One fact to bear in mind when fingering chords in Baroque style is that the bass note will always be on the beat, for it *is* the beat. This means that there is much more time to place the fingers, and no need to grab desperately at the chord or break it before the beat in a pointless attempt to place the *topmost* note on the beat. Depending on the context, then, by using such fingering methods, one can generally approach chordal technique in a far more relaxed way.

Certain Baroque violin techniques are certainly practicable on the modern instrument. For example, I frequently use contracted fingerings, again without moving the thumb, for the same purpose:

It is always better when possible to avoid sliding between slurred half-steps:

It is always preferable to choose a fingering that avoids changing position under a slur, even when it involves jumping to a higher position:

However, in the following example, where a change of position under the slur is inevitable, make use of the half-step between A and B-flat, where the shift is easily disguised:

Intonation

Whereas one must always think horizontally when playing Bach's solo pieces because of the omnipresent polyphony, intonation is to be heard vertically, because each voice relates to the bass line and each melodic note is part of the current harmony. There's nothing radical about the concept of vertical intonation: it is a fact of life in any ensemble situation. String quartet players and woodwind sections in orchestras have to deal with it all the time. In promoting "expressive" intonation, whereby sharps are raised and flats are lowered, our modern training fails to take into account the importance of the harmonic series and the need for pure thirds and sixths, with major intervals narrower and minor wider than we're led to understand. Eighteenth century musicians were trained to hear semitones as major or minor—semitones between notes of different names were major and between notes of the same name minor. Hence C to D-flat was regarded as a major half-step, while C to C-sharp was minor; ergo, C-sharp was considered to be lower in pitch than D-flat, a fact that is easily proven. Try this simple exercise:

Sustain the fingers on the string, listening carefully to each interval to make sure that the sixths, fourths, and thirds are pure. You'll notice that the G-flat is very dissonant with the open A, creating tension, whereas the F-sharp is consonant, noticeably lower and relaxed: as for the semitones, F/G-flat is wide, as is F-sharp/G. Since "expressive" intonation is simply the custom of playing leading notes and minor thirds deliberately out of tune—sharps sharper and flats flatter—it is a pity that students so trained are unaware of the fact, not taught to hear individual notes as parts of harmonic entities. If there were something that might be labeled "expressive" intonation in Baroque music, it would be comparative intervallic relationships such as in the above example: A/G-flat versus A/F-sharp, tension versus relaxation. Paying attention to dissonances and being sensitive to subtle shades of enharmonic difference is an essential element of the interpretative process. Modern concepts of intervallic intonation can pervert the eighteenth-century intention: as an example, the diminished seventh E-flat/F-sharp, in which we are taught to pull the E-flat down and raise the F-sharp, which actually sounds like a consonance, works the opposite way from eighteenth-century language, which creates stronger dissonance by having the notes pull away from each other.[6]

Tuning

There is no easy answer to the question of how best to tune the violin; what is certain, though, is that a violin tuned in perfect fifths is functionally out of tune. One option is to have a pure sixth between G and e' tempering the fifths slightly so that every note on the instrument is perfectly in tune with all four open strings. The problem with this is that the fifths between the open strings are noticeably narrow; if one tunes in perfect fifths, though, chords that include open G and E (C-major and E-minor) will be out of tune. Therefore, there has to be a compromise that minimizes these unfortunate side effects.

This is a complex challenge that confronts those who tune keyboard instruments and one that has resulted historically in a variety of solutions.[7] Simply expressed, the problem is how to narrow intervals so that the C at the end of the circle of pure fifths corresponds in pitch to the one at the beginning. Equal temperament, the blandest, in which all intervals are narrowed by the same amount, has become the most common in our age, but during the Baroque era there were numerous others that satisfied the needs of composers and performers. Early temperaments favored keys with no more than two sharps or flats so as to avoid enharmonic clashes as much as possible. These so-called *meantone* temperaments had a number of pure thirds mixed with others that were painfully dissonant.[8] By Bach's time, though, the degree of inequality had diminished to the point that he could compose the *Well-Tempered Clavier*, his set of Preludes and Fugues in all twenty-four keys, each of which still has its own individuality without his resorting to the use of equal temperament.[9]

---

6. Further evidence of the sophistication of eighteenth-century musicians is to be found in *An Essay on Musical Expression* (1753) by Charles Avison, a prominent English composer and organist, in which he refers to the "expressive use of the quarter-tone" and "the enharmonic scale of the Greeks." You might try playing an enharmonic scale sometime . . .

7. Noteworthy among these was a seventeenth-century harpsichord with split accidental keys and an extra set of strings to allow for enharmonic variation. It was, not surprisingly, an invention soon discarded as being too difficult and time-consuming to keep in tune.

8. Michelangelo Rossi (1601–1656) deliberately exploited this feature in many of his compositions, notably his seventh toccata, which includes a chromatic scale in thirds.

9. As an in-depth discussion of such a vast and complex topic is obviously outside the scope of this book, those wishing to investigate it further are directed to the writings of Mark Lindley and his exhaustive article in *Grove Dictionary*. Another interesting resource is Ross Duffin's excellent book, *How Equal Temperament Ruined Harmony (and Why You Should Care)*.

For our purposes in performing the Sonatas and Partitas, tuning in slightly narrow fifths to reduce the extreme width of the G/E major sixth is most desirable and not difficult to achieve. One quick way is to take the pitch of the octave harmonic on each string and tune the same harmonic at the fifth on the adjacent lower string slightly higher. It is not often, anyway, that one encounters an open-string fifth that needs to be sustained, and besides, fingering fifths on out-of-tune strings is something we have to deal with on a daily basis.[10]

---

10. I direct you also to a more detailed discussion and some exercises in my previous book, *Before the Chinrest*.

Last Words

There are now many recordings of these works—far more than when I was a student—and I am not about to recommend one over another. The choice of a favorite recording is a matter of personal taste, and as I said in my introduction, it's impossible to identify anyone's interpretation as "right." What has changed since my student days is that at that time there were comparatively few reigning virtuosi and only a few few record companies. That was the 1950s, just when the LP was introduced and recording was becoming a far more sophisticated procedure. It was not long before companies began producing recordings of high quality, and when the so-called Early Music movement was launched in Europe in the late 1960s, its pioneers were quick to take advantage of the opportunity. This was the beginning of a revolution during which our ears were assailed by new sounds made on old instruments, sparking a predictable controversy among music lovers. I recall a sarcastic comment by a biased *New York Times* music critic: "This, too, shall pass!" The poor man has been forced to eat his words, for, whether he liked it or not, the revolution has been successful beyond any prediction, and we have long since become accustomed to hearing familiar repertoire performed on the instruments for which it was composed. Besides the modern virtuosi, there are a number of fine performers on historical instruments who have recorded the Sonatas and Partitas, and it is now possible, therefore, to compare radically different approaches to their interpretation.

As I have already observed, it was not my intention in writing this book to proselytize, to seek to convert anyone to the use of a Baroque instrument or even to persuade readers of the validity of my conception, but simply to share my experience as a teacher and performer in hopes that what I have offered may be helpful in making the pieces more accessible. Obviously, I have strong opinions about certain aspects of pedagogy and interpretation, and if I have at times erred on the side of hypercriticism, it is, after all, in the grand tradition of eighteenth-century invective, as anyone who has read Leopold Mozart or Francesco Geminiani will recognize. What's wonderful about music now is the variety of interpretative approach, and there's something for everybody to enjoy according to personal taste or predilection.

Of course, the Sonatas and Partitas are but a small fraction of the amount of music that makes up today's "standard repertoire," and the demands on students' time are such that perhaps only one or two of the pieces will be learned during the formative period. However, their real importance in any violinist's development extends far beyond mere technical craft. There is so much to be gleaned from their careful study that can be applied to other repertoire—truths that can be applied to all music—thereby supporting one's growth as a *musician*.

For me, Bach's music is a source of endless fascination and wonder. I hope that the suggestions I have made in this volume may complement or reinforce your own understanding and appreciation of his extraordinary achievement, or lead you along previously unexplored paths. I wish you joy and fulfillment in your own voyage of discovery.

Bibliography

Avison, Charles. *An Essay on Musical Expression*. London, 1753.

Bach, Johann Sebastian. *Sei Solo à Violino senza Basso accompagnato*. Cöthen, 1720. (Manuscript in Berlin State Library, Preußischer Kulturbesitz, Music Department with Mendelssohn Archive)

von Biber, Johann Heinrich. *Rosenkrantz Sonaten, Passacaglia*. ca. 1675.

von Biber, Johann Heinrich. *Sonatae*. Nuremberg, 1681.

Bismantova, Bartolomeo. *Compendio musicale*. 1677.

Buelow, George J. "Johann Adolph Scheibe." In *Grove Music Online*.

Chew, Geoffrey, and Richard Rastall. "Mensural Notation from 1500." In *Grove Music Online*.

Duffin, Ross. *How Equal Temperament Ruined Harmony (and Why You Should Care)*. New York: Norton, 2007.

Farina, Carlo. *Il quarto Libro delle Pavane, Gagliarde . . . Sonate, Canzon à 2, 4*. Dresden, 1628.

Forkel, Johann Nicolaus. *Über Johann Sebastian Bachs Leben, Kunst und Kunstwerke*. Leipzig, 1802.

Frescobaldi, Girolamo. *Toccate e Partite d'intavolatura di cembalo . . . libro primo*. Rome, 1615.

Fuller, David. "Notes inégales." In *Grove Music Online*.

Garden, Greer. "Double." In *Grove Music Online*.

Geminiani, Francesco. *The Art of Playing on the Violin*. 1751, facsimile (D. D. Boyden, ed.). London: Oxford University Press, 1952.

Ledbetter, David. "Prelude." In *The New Grove Dictionary of Opera*. 2001.

Lindley, Mark. "Tuning." In *Grove Music Online*.

Little, Meredith, and Natalie Jenne. *Dance and the Music of J. S. Bach*. Bloomington: Indiana University Press, 1991.

Marini, Biagio. *Sonate, Symphoniae . . . op. 8*. Dresden, 1626.

Marpurg, Friedrich Wilhelm. *Clavierstücke mit einem practischen Unterricht, i–iii*. Berlin, 1762–1763.

Matteis, Nicola. *Ayres for the Violin*. London, 1676, 1685.

Mattheson, Johann. *Der vollkommene Kappelmeister*. Hamburg, 1739.

Moens-Haenen, G. "Vibrato." In *Grove Music Online*.

Mozart, Leopold. *Versuch einer gründlichen Violinschule*. Augsburg, 1756. Editha Knocker (trans.). London: Oxford University Press, 1948.

Pisendel, Johann Georg. *Solosonate für violine in A-moll*. Dresden, 1716.

Ritchie, Stanley. *Before the Chinrest – A Violinist's Guide to the Mysteries of Pre-Chinrest Technique and Style*. Bloomington: Indiana University Press, 2012.

Rossi, Michelangelo. *Toccate* e *Correnti*. Rome, 1657.

Silbiger, Alexander. "Chaconne." In *Grove Music Online*.

Tarling, Judy. *The Weapons of Rhetoric*. St. Albans, UK: Corda Music Publications, 2013.

Tartini, Giuseppe. *Traité des agrémens de la musique*. Paris, 1770.

Walther, Johann Gottfried. *Musicalisches Lexicon, oder Musicalische Bibliothec*. Leipzig, 1732.

Walther, Johann Jakob. *Hortulus Chelicus*. Mainz, 1688/1694.

von Westhoff, Johann Paul. *Suite pour le violon seul sans basse*. Paris: Mercure galante, 1683.

von Westhoff, Johann Paul. *Solo Partitas*. Dresden, 1696.

Wilson, David. *Georg Muffat on Performance Practice*. Bloomington, IN: Early Music Institute, 2001.

Wolff, Christoph. *The New Bach Reader*. New York: Norton, 1998.

STANLEY RITCHIE is a professor of music at the Jacobs School of Music at Indiana University. He was born and educated in Australia, graduating from the Sydney Conservatorium of Music in 1956. In 1963 he was appointed concertmaster of the New York City Opera, and then served as associate concertmaster of the Metropolitan Opera from 1965 to 1970. In 1975 he joined the Philadelphia String as first violinist and in 1982, accepted his current appointment at Indiana University. He is a leading exponent of Baroque and Classical violin playing whose interest in historical performance dates from 1970. In June 2009, he received Early Music America's highest award, the Howard Mayer Brown Award for Lifetime Achievement in Early Music. In April 2016 he was promoted by the President of Indiana University to the rank of Distinguished Professor.

www.ingramcontent.com/pod-product-compliance
Lightning Source LLC
Chambersburg PA
CBHW081203240426
43669CB00039B/2797